Design Motifs

EDITORIAL SUPERVISION
FOR THE SERIES

Tokyo National Museum
Kyoto National Museum
Nara National Museum
with the cooperation of the
Agency for Cultural Affairs
of the Japanese Government

FOR THE ENGLISH VERSIONS

Supervising Editor
John M. Rosenfield
Department of Fine Arts, Harvard University
General Editor
Louise Allison Cort
Fogg Art Museum, Harvard University

ARTS OF JAPAN 1

DESIGN MOTIFS

by Saburō Mizoguchi

translated and adapted by Louise Allison Cort

New York · WEATHERHILL/SHIBUNDO · *Tokyo*

This book appeared originally in Japanese under the title Monyō *(Design Motifs)* as Volume 29 in the series Nihon no Bijutsu *(Arts of Japan)*, published by Shibundō, Tokyo, 1968.

The English text is based directly on the Japanese original, though some small adaptations have been made in the interest of greater clarity for the Western reader. Modern Japanese names are given in Western style (surname last), while premodern names follow the Japanese style (surname first).

First edition, 1973

Published jointly by John Weatherhill, Inc., 149 Madison Avenue, New York, N.Y. 10016, with editorial offices at 7–6–13 Roppongi, Minato-ku, Tokyo; and Shibundō, 27 Haraikata-machi, Shinjuku-ku, Tokyo. Copyright © 1968, 1973 by Shibundō; all rights reserved. Printed in Japan.

Library of Congress Cataloging in Publication Data: Mizoguchi, Saburō, 1896– / Design motifs. / (Arts of Japan, 1) / Translation of Monyō. / 1. Design, Decorative—Japan. I. Title. II. Series. / NK1484.A1M5813 / 745.4′4952 / 72–89447 / ISBN 0–8348–2700–x (hard) 0–8348–2703–4 (soft)

Contents

Translator's Preface

THIS BOOK SURVEYS THE ORIGINS and development of traditional Japanese decorative motifs. Working within the chronological framework of the Japanese art-historical periods, from the neolithic to the present day, the author selects the representative motifs of the time and discusses their origins, variations, and applications to the various art forms of each era. In those instances where patterns have remained continuously in use over many centuries, the author attempts to show how their characteristics were altered to suit the changing tastes of the successive periods. He adds a separate chapter on traditional textile motifs and family crests, which are in a sense capsulized versions of basic designs.

The author is emphatic in establishing the connection between traditional design motifs and the objects on which they made their appearance, whether they be lacquer ware or ceramics, paper scrolls or architectural fittings. Good decoration cannot be isolated from the objects whose appearance it enhances. The Western reader may well note the paradox that what Western art history has chosen to identify as "decorative arts" the Japanese would insist are "utilitarian arts." Decoration in the West has always been considered of a lesser order than the fine arts, as though it were somehow frivolous or unnecessary. The Japanese attitude toward design and decoration is very different. The very richness and abundance of Japanese decorative motifs may be explained in part by the conviction that their role of ornamenting daily life is a vital one. Any object derives its identity from its use, rather than its presence standing on a shelf or hanging on a wall, and to the Japanese the decoration of the object is as integral to its use as the actual function it serves.

L.A.C.

Introduction

A CULTURED MAN considers with care the appearance of the clothing, furnishings, and utensils he uses, for he realizes that they are but extensions of his own personality. Primitive people are no less concerned with the appearance of their personal belongings and take pains in ornamenting them. Most people today select their possessions with the hope that, in addition to serving the functions for which they were designed, they will be attractive to look at; in the process of selecting a particular object, people often reject many before finding one that pleases them. And yet, overwhelmed by the deluge of standardized patterns and colors that result from mass production, we may fast be approaching a point where fine decoration loses all powers of attraction for us.

Artists and craftsmen throughout Japanese history have applied their skills to the developing of pleasing and meaningful decorative motifs, and they have perfected techniques of carving, painting, lacquering, dyeing, and weaving to give permanent expression to their favorite motifs. Utilizing these designs and techniques, they enhanced the appearance of religious articles as well as the material objects of everyday life, they ornamented every element of their surroundings and embellished every feature of their architecture.

The design illustrated in Plate 55 is perhaps representative of the attitudes of Japanese people toward certain decorative motifs. The picture shows part of the cover of the *Jinki-bon* sutra scroll, one of thirty-three such scrolls presented in 1164 to the Itsukushima Shrine by the powerful Taira family. Commonly known as the Taira Dedicatory Sutras and designated national treasures, these scrolls are an extraordinary treasury of design motifs popular during the Heian Period. Contained in a case that is magnificently decorated in gold and silver the *Jinki-bon* scroll is fastened with a cord braided of threads of five colors. In a purely functional sense, plain white paper would certainly have sufficed for the copying of the sutras contained in the scroll. However, the artists responsible for producing the scrolls preferred to decorate their paper with a profuse variety of patterns and rich, colorful embellishments. In addition, the outer surfaces of the scrolls were covered with glorious ornamentation. Painted in delicate colors is the pattern of flowers contained within a horizontal lattice known as the *kikkō-hanabishi* (foliate diamonds in "tortoise shell" lattice) motif. A favorite design pattern of the Heian aristocracy, the *kikkō hanabishi* in this lovely rendering in gold, silver, and blue on a copper-green ground exhibits a grandeur and formal nobility. Clearly, the artists' motivations for such painstaking decorative efforts go far beyond "mere" decoration. The beauty of the Heian artists' work carries within it all their reverence for the Buddhist scriptures inscribed within the scrolls.

Crafts cannot be excluded from a discussion of decorative motifs. As an object is made, the primary consideration must be its use. What is it for? Where will it stand? Who will use it and what will he put into it? It is questions like these that determine the shape and overall design of the object. When he has finished making the object itself, the craftsman then considers how best to enhance its beauty through ornamentation. For decoration, patterns are essential, and to bring the patterns to life the skilled craftsman has at his fingertips an endless variety of techniques. But the decoration and the technique in which it is executed must be an integral part of the object. Those things that seem to exist only for their decorativeness lose all utility. It is only when the decorative patterns and techniques are perfectly appropriate to the function of the object itself that it acquires its ultimate integrity and is ready to take its place in the life of the user.

This small book attempts to survey, in roughly chronological fashion, the decorative motifs that the Japanese people have admired and used extensively to beautify their lives. As he turns its pages, the reader will quickly come to realize that Japan is a rich treasure house of design. Not only have ancient motifs of native origin been preserved there, but also alien designs from as far away as Europe and the Middle East have been cherished and blended—with limitless ingenuity—with the native patterns. The popularity of certain motifs has remained fairly constant throughout the history of Japanese arts and crafts; others have enjoyed a cyclical popularity, fading out of fashion in one era only to reappear with renewed favor and with ingenious modifications a few decades or a few centuries later. If the variety of Japanese design motifs is wide, the range of applications is even wider. The same patterns, or closely related ones, appear in all the fine arts as well as on textiles, furniture, musical instruments, ceramics, weapons, architectural elements, vehicles of transportation—in short, on any surface where eyes are likely to fall. Given so richly varied a subject, a book of this size cannot aspire to being comprehensive. It is but an introduction to an artistic sensibility that has served to inspire the talents of generations of Japanese artists and has produced objects to delight the eyes of Japanese viewers and of people the world over.

Design Motifs

1

The Dawn of Design
Prehistoric Period (to A.D. 552)

Patterns from the prehistoric period in Japan are the straightforward expressions of an uncomplicated human spirit, directly reflecting the experience of life in those early times. From the early designs of primitive men, drawn from encounters with their environment, developed all the patterns of later, more complex ages.

The native Japanese patterns classified as "prehistoric" fall within the province of archaeology as much as of art history. They appear on the handicrafts, tools, and ritual objects that antedate the advent of Buddhist culture from the Asian mainland in the mid-sixth century. Specifically, the term "prehistoric" applies to those designs which appeared during the several millenia of the Jōmon period (up to c. 200 B.C.), the Yayoi period (c. 200 B.C.–A.D. 250), and the Kofun (Tumulus) period (A.D. 250 to 552), encompassing the neo-lithic, bronze-iron age, and the protohistoric cultures of Japan. The designs dating from this dawning of Japanese culture formed the matrix for the imported Buddhist motifs of the Asuka (552–645) and Nara (645–794) periods. Among these earliest patterns are not a few which continued, through numberless transformations of shape and composition, to preserve their decorative and spiritual vitality for the people of succeeding ages. Even today, their extreme simplicity evokes a direct and immediate response.

Jōmon Period

The fantastic shapes and patterns of the ceramic vessels and ritual figurines of the Jōmon period are nothing short of astonishing. The powerful designs on

1. *Impressed and raised rope patterns. Earthenware vessel; middle Jōmon period. Tokyo National Museum.*

2. *Spiral pattern. Earthenware vessel; middle Jōmon period. Idojiri Archeological Hall, Nagano Prefecture.*

the pots seem to boil up on the surfaces of their dynamically swelling shapes. Additional decoration is also frequently added around the rims of the pots in wild explosions of pattern. A complete explanation of the cultural sources out of which the Jōmon patterns were born has yet to be made, although it seems certain that they must be related in one way or another to continental Asian cultures. At the same time, they were deeply rooted in the environment of the Japanese islands and in the livelihood of the people. These early Japanese were hunters and fishers, and they fashioned from clay, the easiest of all materials to obtain and to work by hand, the utensils they needed for their daily cooking and storage. Before firing the ware, they added simple designs on the exterior surfaces of the vessels both to ornament them and, at the same time,

to complete the vessels' shape. The tools used included strings or cords twisted together or wrapped around a stick, sections of bamboo, and shells. The rope-like impressions produced by the cords are so prevalent on the pottery of the time that they gave their name (*jōmon* means "cord pattern") to the entire culture.

More elaborate raised patterns were produced by affixing thin coils of clay to the surface of the vessels. In combination with the incised and impressed patterns the relief bands created a lively, sculptural texture. It is not difficult to imagine that the impressed rope patterns echo baskets made of braided vines, while the raised patterns imitated in clay the twisted vines used to construct the decorative edges and other ornamentation on such baskets.

Along with the functional but violently expressive

3. *Spirals and "running line" motifs. Earthenware vessel; Yayoi period. Tokyo National Museum.*

4. *Relief panels on a cast bronze ritual bell, showing human figures, animals, insects, a storehouse; Yayoi period. Agency for Cultural Affairs of the Japanese Government.*

vessels were made clay figurines in human or animal shapes called *dogū*. These probably served some function in religious rituals, and were also adorned with sharp, clear patterns.

Although Jōmon objects have been unearthed all over Japan, the multitude of shapes and designs they exhibit can be classified by reference to certain vessels excavated from sites in the central area of Honshū island (Plates 1, 2). The patterns on these pieces are characterized by a marked preference for oblique lines and every variety of spiral and coil. Also frequently seen are diamonds, circles, curved lines, zigzag *yamagata* (mountain shape) lines, herringbone patterns, and human figures. The patterns occur primarily as parts of continuous schemes of complex surface ornamentation. The special techniques of creating the designs

have given their names to certain characteristic patterns: *yori-ito* (twisted string), *oshigata* (impressed shapes), *kaigara* (impressed patterns made with the edge or full face of a scallop shell), and *jokon* (striations made with the edge of the shell). Despite a great range of regional variation, all Jōmon pieces share the same vigor and forcefulness.

Yayoi Period

Following the several thousand years' duration of the Jōmon cultures, the introduction from the continent of rice cultivation gave rise to the Yayoi culture based on this new means of livelihood. Design motifs of the very end of Jōmon continued for a time, but inevitably, as the more settled mode of existence of

5. *Zigzag or "mountain shape" motif. Earthenware vessel; late Yayoi period. Tokyo National Museum.*

6. *Triangle pattern. Wall painting; Kofun period. Daibō tumulus, Kumamoto Prefecture.*

the new agricultural society gained prevalence in Japan, a new type of pottery made its appearance. Whether Yayoi pottery was a development of earlier native styles, possibly influenced by foreign importations, or whether it was introduced by the actual immigration of foreign peoples has yet to be determined.

In design and character, the quieter pottery of the Yayoi period, noted for the attention paid by craftsmen to formal beauty, is very different from the vigorous patterns of Jōmon ware. Decorative patterns seem to take a subordinate role to form and are reduced to flat motifs rendered in vivid colors. On the whole, the Yayoi pots show a far more rational character than those of the dramatically expressive Jōmon style. In early Yayoi ware, the surface of the pot was simply smoothed with a bamboo scraper. Later, incised de-

signs of twill, sawtooth patterns, arc patterns, four-leaf patterns, and complex linear designs began to appear, together with decoration made by scratching with a comb-like tool (Plates 3, 5).

Special mention must also be made of the introduction from the continent during the Yayoi period of techniques of making bronze and working with iron and other metals. The new metal culture was centered first in Kyūshū and southern Honshū, but in time continental skills spread throughout Japan and produced the characteristic Japanese bronze objects known as *dōtaku* (Plates 4 and 15). These are believed to have been used as ritual bells, and on their surfaces appear geometrical patterns of coils, running-water motifs, lattices, triangles, multiple arcs, and stripes. A characteristic decorative device is the *kesa-dasuki* pattern

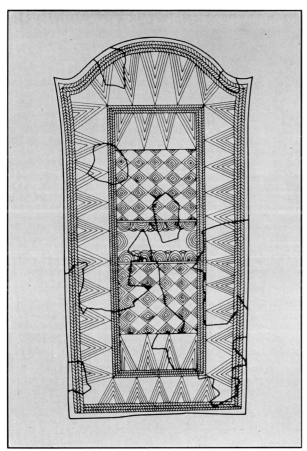

7. *Triangles, diamonds, and concentric arcs. Diagrammatic reconstruction of designs covering a* haniwa *shield; Kofun period.*

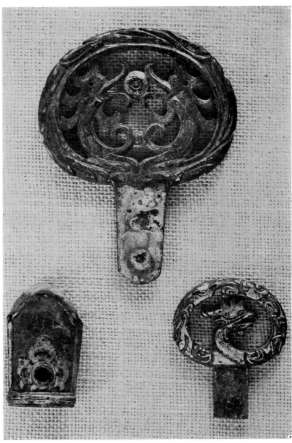

8. *Dragon motif. Gilt-bronze sword pommels; Kofun period. Tokyo National Museum.*

(Plate 15), which was later given this name because of its resemblance to the geometric lattice pattern *(tasuki)* on the *kesa* robes of Buddhist priests. Motifs such as human figures, animals, and birds were drawn from the daily experience of the Yayoi craftsmen and were depicted in fairly literal fashion. Several separate stages in the development of the composition are discernible, the result of an ever-increasing concern for form among artisans of the stable agrarian society. The primitive attempts of the earlier Jōmon craftsmen to fill up a space with decoration gave way to a taste for consciously-ordered ornamentation.

Kofun (Tumulus) Period

From the third through the seventh centuries, magnificent burial tumuli or *kofun* were constructed in central Honshū and Kyūshū for dead emperors and other powerful figures. The decorative motifs that prevailed during the Kofun period may be determined from examining the great variety of objects that have been excavated from the tumuli. Among Kofun relics are the gray, high-fired pottery known as Sue ware, a fusion of native earthenware techniques with the advanced skills of Silla potters from the Korean peninsula. Metalware, influenced by Chinese models, includes arms and armor, horse trappings, mirrors, and personal ornaments, all decorated with advanced techniques of casting, metal carving, and inlay. The motifs appearing on such objects reveal the attention paid by the craftsmen of the time to carefully matching design and technical means of expression.

Generally speaking, a decorative motif changes character according to variations in techniques and materials. Therefore, decoration alone does not insure that an object will be beautiful or will display a particularly striking feeling of life. With the development of this awareness of the complexity and expressive capacity of decorative motifs can be recognized the increasing artistic maturity of the Kofun culture.

The appearance of astonishingly beautiful and moving objects during the Kofun period may be attributed in large part to the importation of outstanding examples of continental craft, which inspired the development of native styles and the mastery of techniques. Decorative motifs became exceedingly complex. Metalwares, for example, were often ornamented with Chinese-inspired designs such as dragons (Plate 8) and the four directional divinities (green tiger of the east, white tiger of the west, red phoenix of the south, black snake-tortoise of the north). Other motifs included human figures, horses and carts, human dwellings, *magatama* (large, comma-shaped semiprecious stones) and arcs, four-petaled flowers, apricot-leaf shapes, vines, phoenixes, pairs of animals, and bird and animal combinations. There are also complex patterns that combine animals, phoenixes, or flowers with the *karakusa* vine-scroll motif. From the sixth century onward, *karakusa* patterns based on honeysuckle vines became widely popular. Later,

during the succeeding Asuka and Nara periods, they formed the basis of the honeysuckle motif commonly used in decorating Buddhist arts.

By contrast, the designs which appear on the faces and clothing of the *haniwa* clay tomb sculptures of the Kofun period are incised or painted in simple color schemes (red predominating) and simple combinations of circles, triangles, and arcs. Since historians doubt that tatooing was prevalent at the time, the designs on the faces of *haniwa* were probably intended purely as decoration and not as literal representations of contemporary custom.

In the painted tombs of Kyūshū are to be seen abundant examples of designs executed in incised lines with mineral pigments including red, yellow, white, blue, green, and black. Among these decorations appear triangle shapes, zigzag "mountain shape" lines, diamonds, single or concentric circles, spirals and fern-like *warabi-de* leaf motifs. Complex patterns based on triangles are the most frequent (Plates 6 and 7). Possibly they were not intended simply as decoration but may also have contained symbolic significance.

These then are the patterns which developed during the dawn of Japanese culture: the direct and powerful Jōmon patterns, the carefully constructed formal Yayoi patterns, and the designs of the Kofun period incorporating the traditions and characteristics of continental styles.

2

Buddhist Motifs
Asuka Period (552-645)

Buddhism reached Japan in the mid-sixth century. From its origins in India roughly one thousand years earlier, the doctrine had passed through Central Asia into China before crossing to Japan by way of the Korean peninsula. Lingering long in the various countries through which it made its way, Buddhism carried with it to Japan an accumulation of local crafts and artistic traditions from the various far-flung cultures of Asia. Not surprisingly, the decorative motifs of the Buddhist arts also reveal the influence of the cultures and geographic areas in which the religion flourished before reaching Japan.

During the Asuka period, Buddhism won numerous devout adherents in Japan, the most eminent of whom was Shōtoku Taishi, prince-regent during the reign of the empress Suiko (592–628). Enthusiastically encouraged by the court, the religion flourished in the Yamato plain around what is today the city of Nara. The comparatively primitive Japanese of the time must have been deeply impressed with the glorious Sui-T'ang continental culture that came to Japan in the wake of Buddhism, for in a rather short time the art, thinking, and social structure of the Yamato area was totally remodeled along Chinese lines. The greatest remaining monument of the new Japanese culture of the Asuka period is the Hōryū-ji temple and monastery built by Suiko and Shōtoku Taishi early in the seventh century. The patterns that are still to be seen on the sculpture and other arts in the temple and in the architectural details of the main hall, the interior gate, the

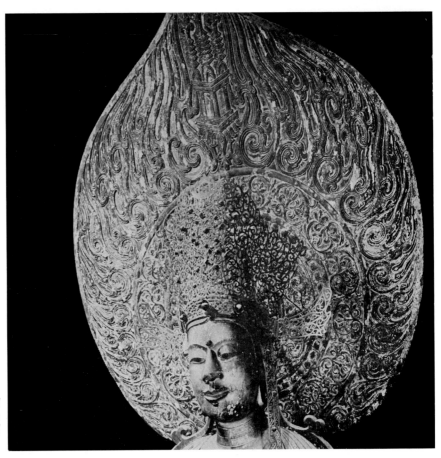

9. *Honeysuckle motif. Halo and crown, gilt-wood image of Guze Kannon; Asuka period, national treasure. Hōryū-ji, Nara.*

five-story pagoda, and other remaining structures provide eloquent testimony to the magnificent flowering of Sino-Japanese culture during the Asuka period.

In general, the arts and architecture of Asuka were strongly influenced by the styles of the Six Dynasties period (c. 222–589) in China, as modified by their passage through the Korean peninsula. Without question, the single most significant decorative motif of the period is the so-called *nindō-mon* or honeysuckle pattern.

The Honeysuckle Motif

The honeysuckle motif, the key design pattern of the Asuka period, is believed to have originated in Greece and migrated slowly across Asia as a truly international pattern. At the Hōryū-ji, it appears on the halo of the bronze Shaka Triad (dated 623) in the main hall, on the diadems of the attendant figures on the main altar, and on the halo of the standing figure of the bodhisattva Kannon known as the Guze Kannon (Plate 9). Elsewhere in the Hōryū-ji, the honeysuckle motif figures in the halos of the angels in the canopy above the central Triad, on the images of the Guardian Kings of the Four Directions, and on a tapestry representing the Guardian Kings.

The pattern receives its richest and most varied treatment, however, on a famous miniature shrine built in the form of a palace building. The shrine is known as the Tamamushi Shrine because the openwork metal edging of its pedestal was originally inlaid with the iridescent wing sheaths of thousands of *tamamushi* beetles. A model of pure Asuka architectural style, the

10. *Honeysuckle motif. Panel of the Tamamushi Shrine; Asuka period, national treasure. Hōryū-ji, Nara.*

11. *Honeysuckle motif. Pedestal of the Tamamushi Shrine; Asuka period, national treasure. Hōryū-ji, Nara.*

shrine is set on a tall pedestal and a wide base. The honeysuckle pattern is applied in colored lacquer to the altar within the shrine (Plate 10) and to the lotus-petal borders on the upper and lower edges of the pedestal (Plate 11). It also appears in the pierced design of the gilt bronze edging.

Bearing a strong resemblance to the metalwork on the Tamamushi Shrine is the bronze ritual canopy, which numbers among the greatest treasures of the Hōryū-ji (Plate 12). On the banner, fluent honeysuckle-motif arabesques frame the central panels in which angel-musicians and lions are depicted. In other Asuka temples, the same honeysuckle motif is to be seen on the roof tiles of the Hokki-ji, a subsidiary temple of the Hōryū-ji; in the brocade tapestry depicting scenes of paradise in the Chūgū-ji nunnery; and in the nimbuses of the small bronze figures from the Hōryū-ji commonly known as the Forty-Eight Bronze Buddhas. Other examples of the honeysuckle motif adorning Asuka and Nara art and architecture are too numerous to mention.

Long before its arrival in Japan, the honeysuckle pattern was a favorite design motif in Greece and the Middle East. Moving gradually eastward through Persia, India, and Central Asia, it appeared in China and in the Korean kingdoms. Examples of the motif are to be found in the stone sculpture in the cave temples at Yunkang and Lung-men in northwest China and in the wall paintings in the Great Tomb at Kangso in Korea (Plate 14). The Japanese name for honeysuckle is *nindō*, and the most common Japanese variety of the plant (*Lonicera japonica*) blooms in profusion in

12. Angels, lions, and honey-suckle karakusa. *Section of gilt-bronze ritual canopy (shown in reverse silhouette at left); Asuka period, national treasure. Tokyo National Museum.*

13. *Honeysuckle* (Lonicera sempervirens), *the plant which may have served as the model for the popular Asuka-period design motif.*

the fields behind the Hōryū-ji. However, the flower which appears in the Asuka patterns is probably the *tsukinuki nindō* (*Lonicera sempervirens*), whose heart-shaped leaves and funnel-shaped flowers, arranged like spokes around the stem, show a striking similarity to the honeysuckle motifs on the various treasures of the Hōryū-ji and other Asuka temples (Plate 13).

The honeysuckle motif is sometimes referred to as the "palmette" pattern. As such it may well be based upon the leaf of the hemp palm, with its symbolic connotations of victory and triumphal glory. A common motif in the Orient since ancient times, the hemp palm would have been a familiar source for the pattern. On the other hand, the motif may have developed from an entirely independent inspiration and only subsequently acquired the names "honeysuckle" or "palmette" from its incidental resemblance to those plants.

Whatever its origins, the honeysuckle motifs shows a rhythmical fluidity in its composition and a formal, repetitive beauty in its shape. Its arrangement can vary to adapt comfortably to any given area or contour, and its component parts lend themselves to endless variation. In the Tamamushi Shrine alone, the honeysuckle appears on the shrine as flowers enclosed by heart-shaped tendrils, on the petals of the lotus borders on the pedestal as individual blooms, and on the metal embellishment as scrolling vines (*karakusa*) and a heart-shaped version of the flower. Elsewhere it takes still other forms: in *karakusa* format with its palm-shaped leaves ranged to each side of the vine; in rows of left-

14. Honeysuckle motif. Wall painting at the Great Tomb at Kangso; Koguryo Kingdom (late sixth century). Korea.

handed scrolls or right-handed scrolls only; in pairs of bands meeting in a peak, as often found on the nimbuses of statues.

Although the use of the honeysuckle motif diminished rapidly after reaching its greatest popularity in the Asuka and Nara periods, it never vanished altogether from Japanese design. Its silhouette reappears in the *hōsōge karakusa* motifs of the early Heian period (Plates 39, 45) and in more stylized form in many later motifs.

While the honeysuckle motif was unrivaled during the Asuka period, numerous other patterns introduced from the continent were being used by Japanese craftsmen and designers. Among them were bird and beast motifs, lotus, clouds, four-petaled flowers and four-leaf patterns. The enormous enthusiasm for these exotic patterns cannot be explained merely as part of the contemporary craze for foreign ideas and imported arts and styles. The patterns established themselves at the center of Japanese culture together with the religious doctrine of Buddhism with which they were so closely associated.

15. Tasuki *motif. The* tasuki *or "sawtooth" design is of uncertain origin, but dates well back into Japanese prehistory, making it one* ▷ *of the oldest extant motifs. On this* dōtaku *(bronze ritual bell) it ornaments the bands surrounding sections of whirlpool and lattice motifs. Yayoi period. Tokyo National Museum.*

3

Flowering of Design

Nara Period (645-794)

During the Asuka period, Chinese cultural influences reached Japan only indirectly, passing first through the Korean peninsula. But with the establishment of T'ang rule in China, direct communication via diplomatic envoys and trade was established between China and Japan. Cultural transmission became a more immediate, intense, and vital process, and the new Japanese capital city, built at Nara in 710 on the Chinese model, became a receptive outpost for the rich and expansive T'ang culture.

Buddhism continued to expand and develop on the foundations laid during the previous period. The enthusiastic program of temple construction carried out in and around Nara encouraged a remarkable development in the decorative arts and in the making of ritual objects for temple use. Inspired by the T'ang example, the numbers and variety of ornamental motifs multiplied rapidly.

Shōsōin Patterns

There is no better introduction to the design motifs that flourished during the Nara period in Japan than an examination of the art treasures preserved in the Shōsōin. In 756, on the forty-ninth day after the death of the emperor Shōmu, his widow Empress Dowager Kōmyō dedicated to the Great Buddha of the Tōdai-ji temple, which her husband had built, over six hundred objects that had been among the late emperor's personal effects. These treasures of the Nara court were placed

16. *Flowers, birds, butterflies, and clouds (radial arrangement). Back of bronze mirror; Nara period. Shōsōin, Nara.*

17. *Hōsōge motif. Back of bronze mirror, with mother-of-pearl and precious stone inlay; Nara period. Shōsōin, Nara.*

in the Shōsōin repository, a large storehouse built within the grounds of the Tōdai-ji. Accompanying the gift were detailed catalogues which provide a uniquely complete and accurate record of the original contents of the Shōsōin. Later, documents, court records, tax books and records of land tenure were kept in the Shōsōin, and additional memorial offerings, gifts, and purchases swelled the number of Shōsōin treasures. All were duly listed and catalogued. Among all the objects in the Shōsōin, those dedicated by Empress Kōmyō are testimony to the superb level of artistic achievement attained by the Buddhist culture in Nara by the mid-eighth century. Some objects were actually imported from the continent, many from China and others from as far west as Persia. Other objects were

made by master-craftsmen from China or Korea who had immigrated to Japan or by native craftsmen working under their supervision. Among the wide variety of motifs found on these objects may be detected both designs of direct Chinese inspiration and others that seem to show indirect influence.

The abundance of decorative motifs and the imaginative variety in their application to the objects in the Shōsōin are apparent even in the following list of major motifs:

- GEOMETRIC MOTIFS: Triangles (arranged in rows in a sawtooth pattern), diamonds, stripes, lattices of intersecting lines, rows of dots, hexagons (in the *kikkō* or "tortoise shell" motif), checkerboards (called *ishi-datami* or "paving stone" motifs), four-

18. Honeysuckle karakusa and lotus motifs seen in the decorations of the supremely beautiful Amida Triad in the small Shrine of the Lady Tachibana. A lotus pond and leaves are represented by fluid lines covering the floor of the shrine, and the lotus motif reappears amid the lovely linear angles on the screen backdrop. The central nimbus is comprised of a large lotus form, encircled by a band of honeysuckle karakusa. Nara period; national treasure. Hōryū-ji, Nara.

19. Hōsōge motif with human figures. Imaginary hōsōge flowers are added to the common karakusa motif of scrolling vines to surround ▷ a scene of a dancing child and two youthful musicians. The hōsōge-karakusa pattern also serves as a border around the lid of this sapanwood box decorated with gold and silver pigment. This T'ang-inspired box is representative of Nara taste. Facsimile in the Tokyo National Museum, based upon a Nara-period original in the Shōsōin Collection, Nara.

20. *Facing deer (symmetrical arrangement). Section of screen; hemp with polychrome stencil-dyed decoration; Nara period. Shōsōin, Nara.*

petal floral shapes, feather shapes, and wave designs

- CELESTIAL MOTIFS: Clouds, mist, sun, and moon
- NATURAL MOTIFS: Landscapes, running-water patterns, rocks, cliffs
- FLORAL MOTIFS: Peony, lotus, hemp palm, Chinese date palm, honeysuckle, acanthus, plantain, grape, pomegranate, chrysanthemum, pine, plum, bamboo, ivy, lily, wisteria, and indeterminate leaves and fruits
- ANIMAL MOTIFS: Peacock, parrot, mandarin duck, chicken, wild goose, duck, pheasant, and small birds; lion, tiger, camel, sheep, reindeer, elephant, rhinoceros, monkey, deer, horse, and fox; butterfly and dragonfly; fish and tortoise
- MYTHOLOGICAL MOTIFS: *Kirin* (a fabulous animal of composite form with wings, long neck, and a sin-

gle horn), the four directional divinities, the twelve animals of the zodiac, phoenixes, flower-eating birds, *karyōbinga* (fantastic bird with bell-like voice that dwells in the Buddhist paradise), winged horses, dragons, *hōsōge* (imaginary Buddhist floral pattern), *karakusa,* auspicious flowers, and sacred trees

- HUMAN-FIGURE MOTIFS: Mounted hunters, charioteers, acrobats, musicians, dancers, game players, children, wizards, and angels
- MOTIFS FROM DAILY LIFE: Musical instruments, utensils for eating and drinking

In the arrangement of these and other motifs, the objects display creative and accomplished use of both simple and highly complicated systems of composition.

- SYMMETRICAL ARRANGEMENTS, FORMAL AND IN-

21. *Phoenix motif.* Nishiki *brocade facsimile; original from Nara period. Shōsōin, Nara.*

22. *Diamond motif. Chest with marquetry ornamentation; Nara period. Shōsōin, Nara.*

FORMAL: In the formal arrangement, the right and left halves of the design are mirror images of each other (Plate 24). In the informal compositions, the two halves of the design vary slightly although the overall impression is balanced (Plate 25). In the decoration of the Shōsōin treasures, the systematic and more intellectual mood of formal symmetry predominates.

• RADIAL ARRANGEMENTS: A flower or bird forms the center of a radiating design which can be extended and expanded indefinitely (Plate 16).

• REVOLVING ARRANGEMENTS: Within a circular area, floral *karakusa* or pairs of birds are disposed so as to give the feeling that the design revolves clockwise or counterclockwise (Plate 23). The outstanding example is the design of two parrots trailing strings of jewels in their beaks, decorating the back of a famous banjo-like musical instrument called the *genkan*.

• SCATTERED ARRANGEMENTS: A combination of various motifs scattered over the surface of an object in a regular (Plate 21) or random fashion.

• PICTORIAL ARRANGEMENTS: Natural scenes formalized into decorative motifs in which the pictorial quality still predominates (Plate 19).

Together with these major types of composition, there are instances of lining up dissimilar motifs in a row (Plate 28) or grouping solid bands of patterns in straight lines (Plate 22) or concentric circles (Plate 17).

The above systems of composition occasionally occur in isolation, but far more frequently they are assembled in complex designs too numerous to list here.

23. Butterflies and floral karakusa *pattern. On the inner surface of this box lid are depicted butterflies amid a red, white, purple, and indigo floral* karakusa *pattern. The design, in its symmetry and revolving arrangement, is typical of the Nara style. Facsimile in the Tokyo National Museum of a Nara-period box preserved in the Shōsōin Collection, Nara.*

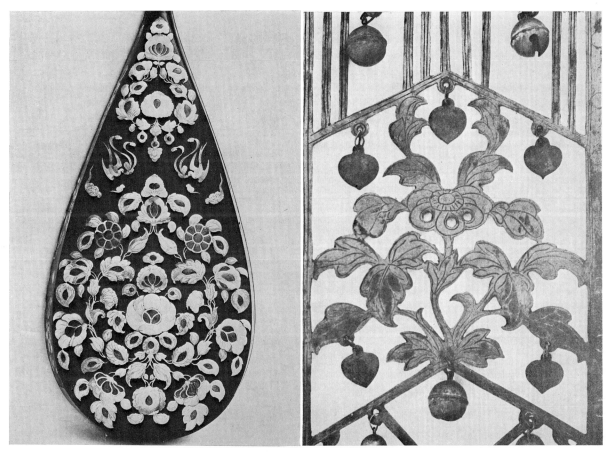

24. Hōsōge *motif (symmetrical arrangement). Back of a five-string* biwa, *red sandalwood with mother-of-pearl and tortoise-shell inlay; Nara period. Shōsōin, Nara.*

25. Hōsōge *motif (symmetrical arrangement). Openwork bronze ritual banner; Nara period. Shōsōin, Nara.*

Underlying such decorations on the Shōsōin treasures is a sense of the designer's keen eye. He has skillfully selected certain motifs from nature and reproduced them in such a fashion as to create a pleasing design. In representations of animals, the characteristics of the particular species are usually subtly accented in order to heighten their quality of vitality (Plate 20). There is never a false touch in the refined placement and overall composition of the ornamentation.

Moreover, the designers of the Shōsōin treasures never forgot that their motifs were intended to ornament functional objects. Their priorities were how best to arrange the design in order to enhance the appearance of the object, and which technique to use in order to express most fully the potential effect of the design. They were never indecisive in their selection of color combinations, and were not afraid to employ highly complex techniques. One such technique called *ungen-saishiki,* after a weaving technique, involved gradations of the same color or combinations of colors placed side by side to create a rich overall effect (as in the gradations of red in the petals of the flowers in Plate 23). Another complicated coloring technique, called *fuse-saishiki,* used patterns or polychromy veiled by a transparent overlay covering of tortoise-shell or crystal. Such techniques typify the designer's resolve to create a beautiful object through the unity and harmony of design and craft. Both the *ungen-saishiki* and *fuse-saishiki* techniques continued in use well into the succeeding Heian period, but were

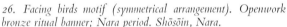

26. Facing birds motif (symmetrical arrangement). Openwork bronze ritual banner; Nara period. Shōsōin, Nara.

27. Facing birds motif (symmetrical arrangement). Fragment of woven textile. Persia.

adapted to the spirit of the new age, gradually losing their exotic flavor and reflecting native Japanese taste to an increasing degree.

The Influence of T'ang Culture

Design motifs of the Nara period, with those decorating the objects in the Shōsōin recognized as their most exquisite expression, owed much to the inspiration of the arts of T'ang China. The T'ang empire stretched far across western Asia, and in its cosmopolitanism it absorbed influences of the Sassanian empire in Persia, of the Byzantine civilization and the Eastern Roman empire, and of other regions of Central Asia through which passed the fabled trade route known as the Silk Road. T'ang enthusiasm for exotic motifs

reached its peak in the eighth century, and accordingly, designs appearing on contemporary Shōsōin treasures mirror not only the culture of China and of nearby countries such as Silla in Korea and Po-hai in eastern Manchuria, but also the cultures of western Asia and even the Mediterranean world. Examples of such international motifs include the honeysuckle, hemp palm, coconut palm, acanthus, and grape. Other motifs based on animals not known in the Far East include tigers, lions, camels, rhinoceros, parrots, and peacocks. Exotic human figures from western Asia appear dressed in strange clothing and distinguished by odd faces with large noses and red hair. Similarly, antecedents for the systems of composition seen on the Shōsōin objects are to be found in the arts of various areas of western Asia. Particular mention should be

28. Bird, flower, and animal motifs. Front (right) and back (left) of an ivory foot-rule; Nara period. Shōsōin, Nara.

29. Hōsōge karakusa pattern. Lacquer box with litharge painting; Nara period. Shōsōin, Nara.

made of the overall interlocking circle pattern known in Japan as the *shippo tsunagi* or "seven-jewel motif," after the seven precious substances of the Buddhist scriptures; gold, silver, lapis lazuli, crystal, coral, agate, and pearls. Other such motifs are the *karakusa* as a revolving wreath (Plate 23), and the designs of facing birds (Plates 26, 27) and animals (Plate 20). It was the rich T'ang mixture of native Chinese culture with exotic influences from the West that crossed into Japan during the Nara period. In a sense, the Nara culture that produced the Shōsōin can be called the final station on the international Silk Road.

Other Motifs

Apart from the Shōsōin, other representative design

motifs of the Nara period can be discovered among the paintings, sculpture, and decorative arts in the Hōryū-ji, Tōdai-ji, Tōshōdai-ji, Yakushi-ji, and other great Nara temples and monasteries, as well as on the treasures originally donated to the Hōryū-ji and now in the keeping of the Tokyo National Museum. The major motifs are identical to those found on the objects in the Shōsōin: they include honeysuckle, lotus, *hōsōge*, and grape vines; interlocking circle patterns, fish-scale patterns, and *hōju* (the Buddhist "flaming jewel" motif); seashore motifs, dragons, phoenixes, divinities of the four directions, animal masks, and mythological creatures. Many objects show exceptional design and craftsmanship, while others are noted more for their close connection with continental cultures. In the former category is the incomparably

30. *Honeysuckle motif. Lacquer incense box with litharge painting; Nara period. Shōsōin, Nara.*

31. *Grape* karakusa, *jewel bands, demons, Tortoise and Serpent of the North. Dais of the central image of Yakushi-nyorai; Nara period. Yakushi-ji, Nara.*

beautiful Amida Triad in the Hōryū-ji, contained in what is known as the Shrine of the Lady Tachibana (Plate 18). This shrine was used for the daily devotions of that high-ranking court lady, who was the mother of the Empress Kōmyō and who also dedicated the Tamamushi Shrine to the Hōryū-ji. The sculptural relief of angels in the screen-like backdrop to the triad and the openwork honeysuckle *karakusa* patterns that encircle the central lotus blossom on the nimbus are technically masterful. Each member of the triad, positioned on a lotus-blossom pedestal, appears to have just floated up out of a lotus pond, which is rendered in a relief of beautiful fluid lines covering the floor of the shrine. The canopy roof of the shrine echoes the patterns of fish scales, lotus petals, and polychrome honey-

suckle *karakusa* that appears on the main canopy of the temple itself.

As an example of outlandish grotesquery of certain foreign motifs, the decoration on the base of the bronze image of Yakushi-nyorai, the Buddha of Healing, in the main hall of the Yakushi-ji deserves attention (Plate 31). A formal grapevine *karakusa* pattern girdles the upper portion. Below it and framing representations of queer and primitive nude figures are two bands of geometrical "jewel" motifs, with the divinities of the four directions inserted in the lower band (only one is visible at the center of Plate 31). The grotesque, demonic figures flanking the directional deities are distinctly un-Japanese in appearance. Representations of such gnome-like figures probably

32. Phoenix, drifting clouds, and hōsōge. *Dry-lacquer nimbus for image of Miroku-bosatsu; Nara period. Hōryū-ji, Nara.*

33. Lotus motif. Round rooftiles; Nara period. Tokyo National Museum.

originated in western Asia and traveled via China to Japan, where they represent an extreme in exoticism.

Among the possessions of the Tōdai-ji, the armor on the image of Kōmoku-ten, one of the Four Guardian Kings in the Sangatsu-dō hall, is figured with a rich pattern of interlocking circles, honeysuckle *karakusa,* and lion masks. The central image of the Fukūkensaku Kannon in the same building is graced by outstanding altar decorations and utensils, but none surpasses the boat-shaped openwork halo with its checkerboard arrangement of *karakusa* patterns.

Hōsōge and Peony Motifs

Still another popular motif in the gorgeous panoply

of Nara designs is the so-called *hōsōge* pattern (Plate 32), named not for any actual flower but for an imaginary floral design which appeared as part of the continental Buddhist art culture. The term, as yet a subject of some speculation, literally means "jewel-face-flower." One theory suggests that the *hōsōge* is an idealized version of the *hōrenge* or sacred Buddhist lotus; another asserts that it derives from the *bussōge* or Chinese rose. Neither theory is totally convincing.

Contrary to both these theories, the special characteristics of the *hōsōge* pattern and its continental origins would suggest that it was modeled after the peony in combination with elements of other flowers. Among the types of peony *hōsōge,* one is based upon stylized elements of the peony—flowers, buds, seeds, stalks, and leaves—while other more simplified designs do not include the seeds. Certain other *hōsōge* patterns are based upon single conventionalized peony plants or stalks. In all versions, however, the *karakusa* format predominates. The *hōsōge* motif reached the height of its popularity during the Heian period; during the succeeding Kamakura period, it took on an increasing similarity to the clearly identifiable peony *karakusa* (Plates 34, 47, 48, 52).

Other motifs based upon the peony combine it with lotus, grapes, honeysuckle, and other flowers in complex patterns forming magnificent imaginary floral designs. Later motifs called *zuika* (auspicious flower) or *karahana* (Chinese flower) were based upon certain types of *hōsōge* designs. There are also patterns of four-petaled or multi-petaled flowers clearly not of the peony type which nonetheless fall into the *hōsōge* category, probably simply for the convenience of classifying an otherwise unidentifiable floral pattern. There are also other floral motifs, which seem to resemble chrysanthemums, acanthus leaves, palmette, *bussōge*, and pomegranate, but which nevertheless are included in the *hōsōge* category.

The peony, which may well have inspired the wide range of *hōsōge* patterns, is a flower native to Asia. In China it symbolizes wealth and honor and was often referred to as the "king of flowers." The peony is known to have been growing in the Hsi-yüan garden in Loyang during the early Sui dynasty (A.D. 581–618), and during the T'ang it was widely cultivated and highly esteemed. The popularity of the flower gave birth to the peony motifs, which in turn were transmitted to Japan and established in the repertoire of Japanese design. Tradition has it that the first actual peony plant was brought to Japan during the reign of the Emperor Shōmu (724–49) and was planted in Nara, but the name of the plant does not appear in written records until the Heian period and the actual extent of cultivation of peonies in Nara Japan cannot be ascertained. It seems most likely, therefore, that the peony motif was incorporated in Nara art only through second-hand knowledge gained through examining imported objects. Some scholars have even ventured to say that any object bearing the peony motif and dating from the Nara period must have been of foreign manufacture.

4

Development of a Native Style
Heian Period (794-1185)

As the intensity of Japanese cultural borrowing from T'ang China diminished, partly as a result of the cessation of official embassies to the T'ang court, the all-pervading Chinese influence upon the arts gradually gave way to an increasingly original and unmistakably Japanese style. Heralding this new era was the transfer of the capital in 794 from Nara to Heian-kyō (modern Kyoto), specifically for the purpose of renewing the vitality of the country. The winds of change blew gently through the world of design as well, although some time was to pass before distinctly innovative motifs appeared. Thus, the early Heian period should be seen as a time of transition, during which design formats were still steeped in the Chinese inheritance from the Nara period but were beginning to evolve toward independent and more authentically Japanese forms of expression.

Designs of the Transitional Period

The design characteristics of the transitional period are clearly to be seen in the patterns that adorn the miniature shrine in the Mandala Hall of the Taima-dera temple in Nara Prefecture. The shrine was made in 763 to house a tapestry representing the Paradise of Amida which is the chief object of worship in the temple. The surfaces of the shrine are decorated in gold and silver tempera with Nara-type motifs including *hōsōge*, butterflies, phoenixes, long-tailed birds, pheasants, ducks, sun and moon, and landscapes (Plate 34).

34. Hōsōge motif. Gold and silver tempera decoration on Taima mandala shrine; Heian period. Taimadera, Nara Prefecture.

35. Lotus karakusa motif. Inlaid lacquer sutra case; Heian period, national treasure. Nara National Museum.

The eave boards were originally ornamented with sheets of gold leaf cut in the shapes of *hōsōge* and jewels, phoenixes, long-tailed birds, parrots, and adoring angels floating on clouds. Today, even though most of the decoration has peeled off, the gold leaf has left a clear impression of the original design. The same motifs and their techniques are also found on many of the Shōsōin treasures, but these later versions have lost their earlier formality and feeling of fullness. Their new simplicity and refinement shows a distinct shift of emphasis away from the Nara taste.

In the Ninna-ji temple in Kyoto there is preserved a lacquer box designed to contain the thirty volumes of sacred scriptures which the renowned Buddhist priest and teacher Kōbō Daishi (774–835) carried back to Japan from China (Plate 39). The inscription on the outside of the cover lists the date of the box as the nineteenth year of the Engi era (919). The inscription itself forms the focal point of the design; around it, in a clockwise rhythm, move *hōsōge karakusa*, kalavinka birds, clouds, butterflies, and birds. Along with the *hōsōge* motif in *karakusa* format, there are single and double tree peonies, grapes, and leaves resembling both peony and lotus. All these motifs follow the models of the previous period, and their arrangement is quite formal. And yet, compared to Nara motifs, these seem somewhat standardized and, while fluent, hardly very powerful.

Hōsōge motifs still deeply colored by the earlier period are also found on a lacquer jewel box in the

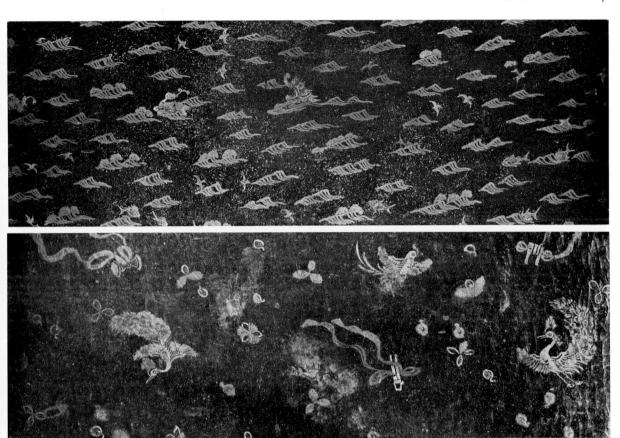

36. *Seascape with waves, birds, fish, and sea monsters. Inlaid lacquer chest; Heian period, national treasure. Kyō-ō Gokoku-ji, Kyoto.*

37. *Peacocks and musical instruments. Cover of an inlaid lacquer sutra box; Heian period, national treasure. Fujita Art Museum, Osaka.*

Ninna-ji, the lacquer box for priests' garments now in the Nezu Museum in Tokyo, and the carved priest's scepter (dated 951) in the Tokyo National Museum. In all these pieces, there is evident a certain urge to depart from the Nara style, even though the *hōsōge* continued to be highly popular as a design motif. The thorough adaptation of this imported motif to a native taste was accomplished after the Fujiwara family rose to absolute power in the mid-Heian period.

Around the same time, there emerged a type of pictorial motif based upon skilled representations of natural landscape. In the seascape on a lacquer garment box in the Kyō-ō Gokoku-ji temple (or Tō-ji) in Kyoto, for example, a fabulous dolphin-like fish called *shachi*, giant tortoises, birds, and waterfowl disport amidst the

choppy waves of a sea that is both fascinating and fearful (Plate 36). This sort of landscape began to appear with increasing frequency after the mid-Heian period in ever more realistic and polished form. Another example is the decoration of a sutra box in the Fujita Museum in Osaka (Plates 37 and 40). The motifs represent important themes from the Lotus Sutra which the box was made to contain, and include bodhisattvas, angels, human figures, clouds, seascapes and coastal scenery, trees, phoenixes, musical instruments, and a scene of the Buddhist flower-scattering ceremony. The motif on the exterior of the cover, consisting of scattered musical instruments, rare birds, and flowers, is exceptionally beautiful. The device of echoing in the ornamental motifs the important stories from the sutra

38. Hōsōge medallions. In these two vertically symmetrical medallions set side by side on a lacquer sutra case, the karakusa *is executed in gold and silver, while the medallion outline is done in gold. The effect is of a textile design carried out in inlaid lacquer. Early Heian period; national treasure. Enryaku-ji, Shiga Prefecture.*

39. Hōsōge, karakusa, karyōbinga, *butterfly, and bird motifs.* ▷ *This lacquer box was made in 919 to hold scriptures supposedly brought to Japan from China by Kōbō Daishi (774–835). The design combines natural motifs with* karyōbinga, *fabulous birds that inhabit the Buddhist paradise. The ornamental arrangement revolves around the central inscription. Gold and silver inlay produce a delicate linear pattern characteristic of the early Heian period. National treasure. Ninna-ji, Kyoto.*

納真言根本阿闍梨空海
入唐求得法文冊子之草

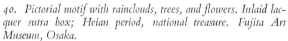

40. *Pictorial motif with rainclouds, trees, and flowers. Inlaid lacquer sutra box; Heian period, national treasure. Fujita Art Museum, Osaka.*

41. *Peacock motif. Gilt-copper ornamental panel on central altar; Heian period, national treasure. Konjiki-dō of Chūson-ji, Hiraizumi.*

to be contained in the box was again attempted in the famous Taira Dedicatory Sutras later in the Heian period. In that case, the decoration is purely Japanese in flavor.

Motifs Related to Jōdo Buddhism

By the time the Fujiwara family took political power in the latter half of the Heian period, new styles had clearly replaced the fading design motifs of Nara. During the so-called Fujiwara period the Kyoto aristocratic culture reached its apogee: this was the period in which Lady Murasaki wrote *The Tale of Genji* and Sei Shōnagon wrote *The Pillow Book*; Fujiwara Michinaga (966–1027), the great nobleman who consolidated the Fujiwara hold over the imperial throne,

built the Hōjō-ji temple in Kyoto, and his son Yorimichi (990–1074) built the lovely Phoenix Hall at the Byōdō-in temple in Uji, south of the city. The Phoenix Hall, completed in 1053, was intended as an architectural representation on earth of the Pure Land paradise of Amida Buddha, the central deity of the Jōdo (Pure Land) sect of Buddhism, which by the eleventh century had won the aristocracy to its mild, gently forgiving doctrines. The interior of the Phoenix Hall is unsurpassed in its opulence (Plate 45). Decoration glorifies every element of the architecture from floor to ceiling, including the canopy and altar for the statues. The techniques used in the construction make use of a great variety of materials, from mother-of-pearl inlay and precious metals to carved and painted wood. The *hōsōge* is the primary motif that unifies the decora-

42. *Facing peacocks. Panel on altar for Buddhist relics; Heian period. Konjiki-dō of Chūson-ji, Hiraizumi.*

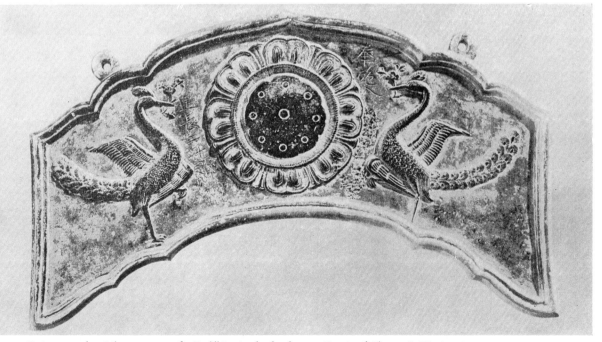

43. *Facing peacocks. Gilt-copper gong for Buddhist rituals; dated 1250. Jizō-in of Chūson-ji, Hiraizumi.*

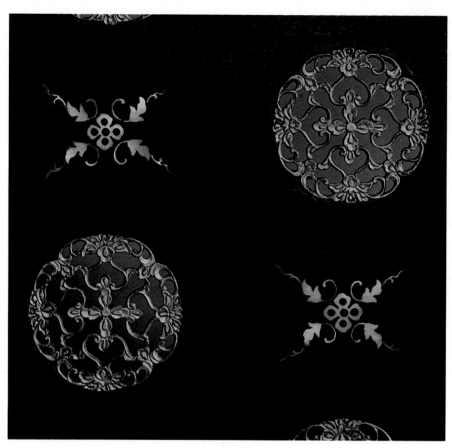

44. Hōsōge pattern. Round hōsōge motifs with the formality of karakusa designs have been applied in gilt openwork on this lacquer inner tray from a Chinese-style chest (Plate 53). The smaller four-petal four-leaf motifs are done in mother-of-pearl inlay. Heian period; national treasure. Kongōbu-ji, Wakayama Prefecture.

45. Hōsōge and lotus karakusa motifs. The lavish original decoration of the interior of the Phoenix ▷
Hall of the Byōdō-in represents Heian design at its peak. Hōsōge karakusa, peony karakusa, rows
of dots, and floral designs cover pillars, ceiling, and other architectural fittings with polychromatic
splendor in the ungen-saishiki technique. Scale model in the Tokyo National Museum of the
Heian-period building in Uji, Kyoto.

46. Karyōbinga *(mythical celestial bird-woman). Decorative panel on octagonal altar; Heian period, national treasure. Daichōju-in of Chūson-ji, Hiraizumi.*

tion of the entire structure. In richly varied compositions and exquisite shapes it adorns the architectural fittings in polychrome pigments. Together with the *hōsōge* intermingle images of the Buddhas and bodhisattvas, auspicious flowers, phoenixes, lotus *karakusa* and interlocking circle patterns in both simple and *karakusa* formats with continuous or scattered layouts. The diversity of the decoration is extraordinary, creating a feeling of immense richness. Even in symmetrical arrangements, precise symmetry is rare. Many of the designs are not totally lacking in Nara influence, but in their glorious opulence, their increased delicacy, and their inventiveness of composition, they exhibit a purely Japanese taste. In the highly colored architectural decoration, the technique known as *ungen-*

saishiki occurs frequently. This technique, involving juxtaposed gradations of color to give an effect of depth to a flat surface, was employed as early as the Asuka period, but no earlier examples can be found to match the richness of the effect in the Phoenix Hall.

The Golden Hall of the Chūson-ji temple was built in 1124 at Hiraizumi, far to the north of Kyoto, by Fujiwara Kiyohira, leader of the northern branch of the Fujiwara family. Beneath the three altars of the sanctuary are the actual graves of the first-generation Kiyohira (d. 1127), his son Motohira (d. 1157), and his grandson Hidehira (d. 1187). The discrepancy of sixty years separating the earliest tomb from the last reveals the evolution of certain design motifs over three generations.

47. Hōsōge karakusa *motif. Dais of miniature shrine with mother-of-pearl inlay; Kamakura period (dated 1243), national treasure. Mandara-dō of Taima-dera, Nara Prefecture.*

48. Hōsōge karakusa *motif. Mother-of-pearl inlay; Heian period, national treasure. Konjiki-dō of Chūson-ji, Hiraizumi, Iwate Prefecture.*

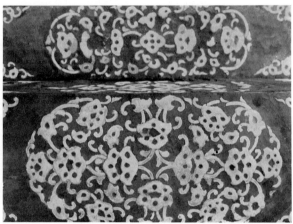

The decoration of the inner sanctuary is carried out primarily in *maki-e* (inlaid lacquer), mother-of-pearl inlay, and metalwork. Its motifs also feature *hōsōge* as the principal theme. Forty-eight images of bodhisattvas in oval medallions, *hōsōge karakusa*, interlocking circles and *ishi-datami* patterns ornament the pillars of the building. To the ornamental panels of the three daises are affixed gilt-bronze plaques of peacocks surrounded by *hōsōge* (Plate 41). On the central dais, *hōsōge karakusa* in gold and silver-gilt frames these plaques, while on the rosewood balustrades *hōsōge* motifs are worked in mother-of-pearl (Plate 48). The *hōsōge* motifs on the pillars and various architectural details show no great difference from those in the Phoenix Hall, but the *hōsōge* on the panels of the daises

bear a close resemblance to an actual peony spray represented in formalized manner. Whether the approach of the *hōsōge* pattern to the likeness of an actual peony can be attributed to the disappearance of exotic cultural influences or to the beginning of peony cultivation in Japan cannot be determined. A reference in *The Pillow Book* of Sei Shōnagon (c. 1002)—"the peonies arranged on the balcony had a strangely Chinese aura"—suggests the lingering association of peonies with the foreign culture, and at the time they must still have been rather rare in Japan. The combination of peony-like *hōsōge* with the equally unfamiliar peacock seems to indicate that the motif was a representation of the imaginary rather than the naturalistic.

The pairing of butterflies and peonies was already

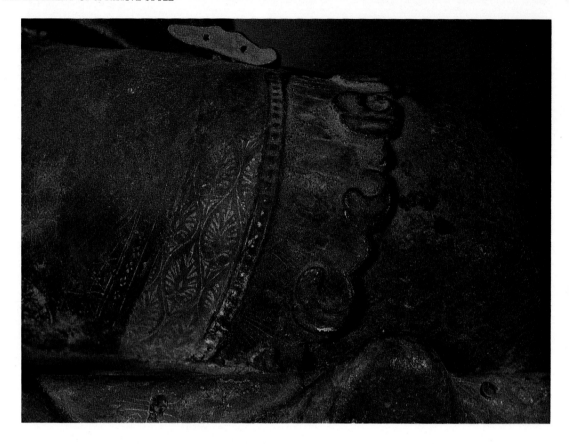

49–50. Kirikane ornamentation. Finely cut sheets of gold leaf applied to a lacquered surface produce the decorative patterns known as kirikane. In these details of a wooden statue of Fugen seated on a white elephant (Plate 54), the skillfully combined motifs include karahana tatewaku (Chinese flowers in undulating patterns), single and clustered chrysanthemums, shippō tsunagi (interlocking circles), and diamond lattice. Heian period; national treasure. Okura Museum, Tokyo.

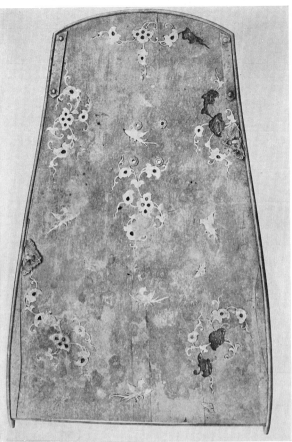

51–52. Pictorial motifs: (left) plovers, rocks, and bamboo grass; (right) hōsōge, butterflies, and parrots. Front and back of flat quiver; Heian period, national treasure. Kasuga Shrine, Nara.

fairly familiar from the decoration of objects in the Shōsōin, but the single instance of this motif in the Chūson-ji Golden Hall occurs on the panel of the central dais. Motifs featuring the peony *karakusa*, naturalistic peony blossoms, or peonies with Chinese lions would not come into fashion until the Kamakura period.

Appearance of Pictorial Motifs

The Heian aristocrats, with their highly cultivated romantic sensibilities, were irresistibly drawn to motifs taken from nature. Rather than imaginary or conventionalized landscapes, they preferred unaffected, almost naive, representations such as that of plovers and marshland that appears on the small Chinese-style lacquer chest in the Kongōbu-ji temple on Mt. Kōya (Plate 53). The entire surface of the box is given over to a charming scene of plovers darting about in the air above marshes where irises are in full bloom. No other motif of the time captures quite so perfectly the characteristic delight of the Japanese in simple natural beauty.

The adoption of certain flowers as ornamental motifs also developed around the middle of the Heian period, and seems to have been an expression of the aristocrats' fascination with the seasonal cycles. Scattered over the inside of the cover of the above-mentioned chest is a rich variety of flowers and grasses. The variety is even greater on the inner surface of the lid of a famous cos-

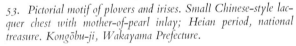

53. *Pictorial motif of plovers and irises. Small Chinese-style lacquer chest with mother-of-pearl inlay; Heian period, national treasure. Kongōbu-ji, Wakayama Prefecture.*

54. Kirikane *decoration. Wood image of Fugen-bosatsu; Heian period, national treasure. Okura Museum, Tokyo.*

metic case in the Tokyo National Museum, the exterior of which is covered with a beautiful design of cartwheels and waves (Plate 62). There are also many examples of this type of floral motif on decorated papers used in the hand-copied editions of the *Anthology of the Thirty-six Poetic Geniuses* produced by the finest calligraphers of Kyoto in the early twelfth century (Plates 58, 63–64).

The cover of the cosmetic box shows cartwheels being soaked in a shallow stream to prevent their drying out. The design is based upon a scene that was apparently of frequent occurrence in the capital. The elements of this everyday scene, curved wheels projecting from the wavy lines of water, create a rhythmical and decorative pattern of great elegance and beauty. The popularity of this humble motif among the aristocracy is clear from its frequent appearance on poetry sheets and on the ornamented papers used for fans, for writing poetry and for copying sutras.

Kirikane Patterns

To increase the dignified beauty of Buddhist sculpture and painting, an ornamental technique known as *kirikane* came into increasing use during the Heian period. It involved applying finely-cut gold leaf to wet lacquer, producing an effect of precise yet lacy patterns that is totally different from that of gold pigment laid on with a brush. Patterns are built up of separate strips, diamonds, triangles, and squares of gold leaf. The

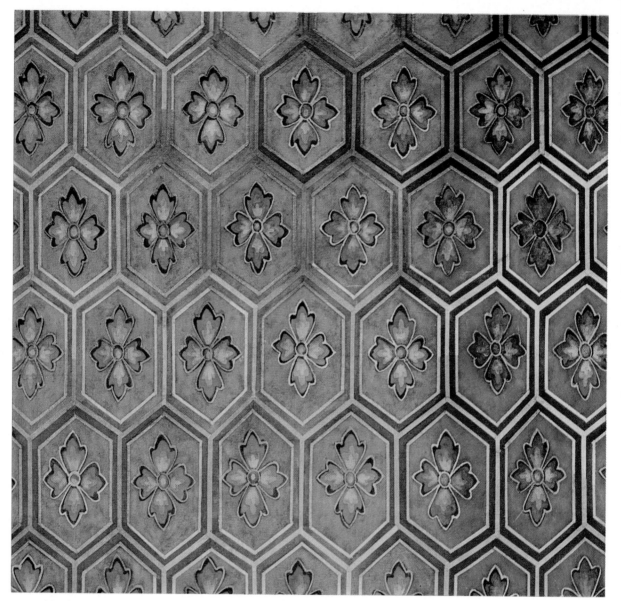

55. Kikkō-hanabishi *pattern. Examples of this design of diamond-shaped flowers enclosed in a hexagonal "tortoise shell" lattice are to be found in the Shōsōin, but the pattern attained its greatest popularity during the Heian period. Here, rendered in blue and gold on a copper-green ground, it enhances the cover of one of the Taira Dedicatory Sutras. Facsimile in the Okura Museum, Tokyo; based on a national-treasure Heian-period original in the Itsukushima Shrine, Miyajima, Hiroshima Prefecture.*

56. Hōsōge karakusa *pattern. The imaginary* hōsōge, *a flower based upon the peony and closely connected with Buddhism, blooms gloriously here on the cover of the* Kanji-bon *scroll in the Taira Dedicatory Sutras. It is represented in brilliant green, blue, and red in a* karakusa *pattern set on a gold ground. Fascimile in the Okura Museum, Tokyo, of the Heian-period original in the Itsukushima Shrine, Miyajima, Hiroshima Prefecture.* ▷

57. Clouds and mist pattern. On this portion of the endpaper of ▷ the Gonnō-bon *scroll in the* Taira Dedicatory Sutras, *clouds and mist drift in a tranquil sky, lit as though by rays from the Buddhist Western Paradise. The sense of color and design are very powerful. The opulence of the entire sutra-copying project is reflected here in the silver leaf, gold particles, and gold dust used in the ornamentation. Facsimile in the Okura Museum, Tokyo, of the Heian-period original in the Itsukushima Shrine, Miyajima, Hiroshima Prefecture.*

oldest examples of the technique occur in simple geometric format on the images of the Guardian Kings of the Four Quarters in the Hōryū-ji and in floral form on the Korean-style *koto* (horizontal harp) in the Shōsōin. The diamond and floral motifs on the Guardian Kings in the Kaidan-in of the Tōdai-ji represent a more sophisticated exploitation of the technique's decorative potential. On Buddhist painting and sculpture of the late Heian period, the use of *kirikane* is almost universal. Outstanding examples of the technique at the peak of its development are, among paintings, the image of Fugen-bosatsu from the Hōjō-ji in Kyoto (now in the Kyoto National Museum) and the painting of Shaka Nyorai in the Jingō-ji near Kyoto; in sculpture, the figure of Fugen seated on his white elephant in the Okura Museum in Tokyo (Plates 49–50 and 54) is a superb example. Special mention must also be made of

the running-water motif worked in *kirikane* on the pedestal of the famous image of Kichijō-ten in the Jōruri-ji temple near Nara. This is the sole extant representation of the running-water motif done in this fashion. During the Kamakura period, the special delicacy and beauty of *kirikane* were lost to stiff formalization as the technique went into decline.

Overlooked Motifs

A discussion of decorative motifs causes one to view certain objects in a different light from that in which they are usually seen. The decorated papers used in the *Anthology of the Thirty-six Poetic Geniuses* (Plates 58, 61, 63–64) in the Nishi Hongan-ji temple and the *Taira Dedicatory Sutras* (Plates 55, 56, 57, 59, 60, 65) in the Itsukushima Shrine on Miyajima island are un-

58. Fusenryō ("floating line") medallions, phoenix, and kara-kusa. *Decorated writing paper for the* Anthology of the Thirty-Six Poetic Geniuses; *Heian period, national treasure.*

59. *Clouds and mist motif. Endpaper of the* Gonnō-bon *scroll of the Taira Dedicatory Sutras; Heian period, national treasure.*

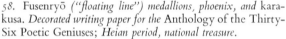

60. *Geometric pattern. Cover of the* Hosshi-bon *scroll of the Taira Dedicatory Sutras; Heian period, national treasure.* ▷

disputed masterpieces of Heian art. They are rarely considered in the context of design, however, and the richness of their ornamentation has too long been overshadowed by their fame as masterful blendings of calligraphy and illustration.

The *Anthology of the Thirty-six Poetic Geniuses* is a collection of the best-known *waka* verses of outstanding poets of the Nara and early Heian periods, including Hitomaro (fl. 680–700), Akahito (d. ?736), Tsurayuki (884–946), and Komachi (fl. c. 850). The anthology was compiled by Fujiwara Teika (1162–1241) and other eminent literary men of the late Heian period, and copied onto specially prepared papers of superb elegance and beauty. Various techniques of collage, including *kasanetsugi* ("layered patches") and

yaburitsugi ("torn patches") created backgrounds of gentle color harmonies and sophisticated design. To these were applied stamped designs and freehand sketches in gold and silver of landscapes, flowers and grasses, and birds and butterflies. Finally, the poems were inscribed in rhythmically flowing cursive script by the finest calligraphers of the day. A single glimpse of the poetry sheets is enough to convey an impression of the whole aesthetic sensibility of the Heian aristocracy. There is a great variety of motifs, including nearly all the favorite themes of the Heian decorators: butterflies, dragonflies, birds, and rabbits; wisteria, pine, willow, maple, plum, cherry, chrysanthemum, autumn flowers and grasses (*akigusa*), gentians, and other seasonal flowers; reeds, pampas grass, bamboo,

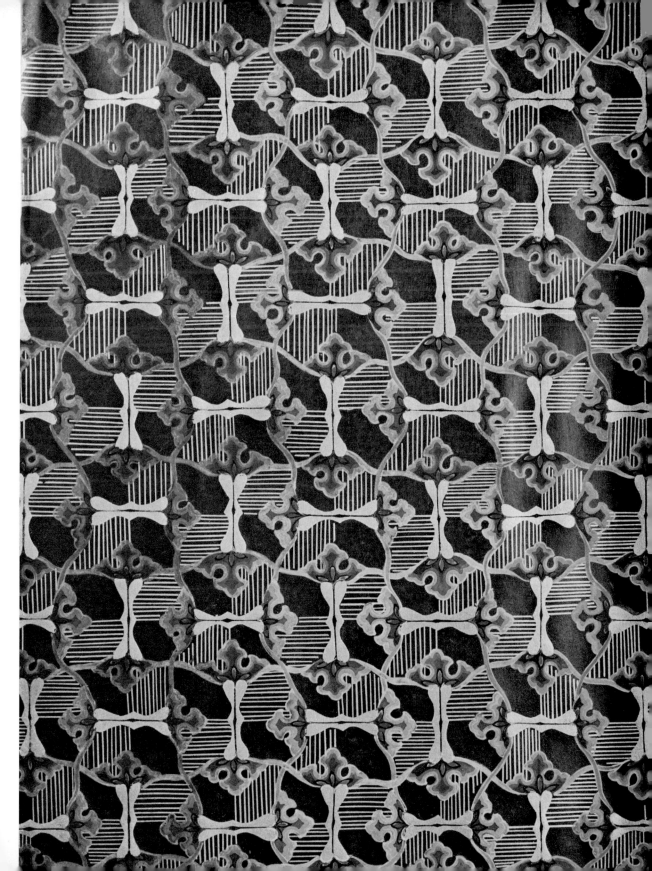

61. *Decorated poetry paper for the* Anthology of the Thirty-six Poetic Geniuses. *This is one portion of the paper used to inscribe the verses of Fujiwara no Motozane. Unique combinations of form and color are achieved by the collage of torn paper. On this surface are drawn branches of leaves, butterflies, and birds, overlaid with bits of gold leaf. At the bottom is added a stylized sketch of cormorants with large pots, which resemble in shape the phonetic symbol for* u; *since* u *is also the name for cormorant, a visual pun in the* ashide *manner is created. Heian period; national treasure. Copy in Nishi Hongan-ji, Kyoto.*

62. *Cartwheels in the stream motif. Apparently, wooden cartwheels had to be soaked periodically to prevent their drying* ▷ *out. The genius of the craftsman who took this common scene and transformed it into a design of great elegance and rhythmical beauty on the cover of a lacquer box is representative of the late-Heian taste for decorative motifs based on everyday objects. National treasure. Tokyo National Museum.*

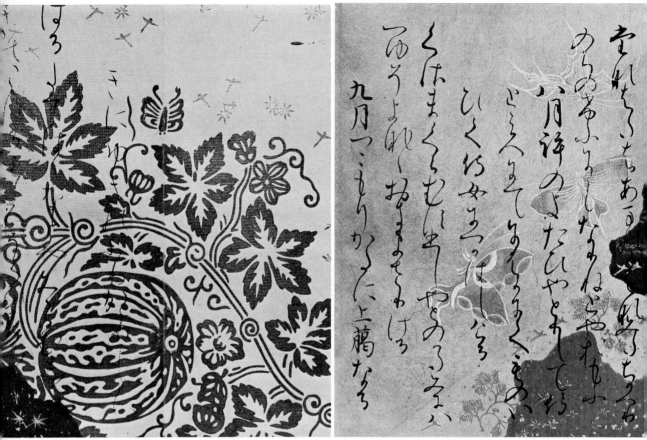

63–64. Butterfly and melon motifs. Decorated writing papers for the Anthology of the Thirty-Six Poetic Geniuses; *Heian period, national treasure. Facsimiles; originals in Nishi Hongan-ji, Kyoto.*

65. Lotus karakusa *pattern. Cover of the* Shinge-bon *scroll of the Taira Dedicatory Sutras; Heian period, national treasure. Facsimile ▷ in Okura Museum, Tokyo; original in Itsukushima Shrine, Hiroshima Prefecture.*

66. *Scattered butterflies, birds, flowers, and grasses. Heian designers delighted in representing the varied flowers and grasses of the four seasons. This design covering the inner surface of the lid of a lacquer cosmetic box is worked in gold, silver, and mother-of-pearl inlay; Heian period, national treasure. Tokyo National Museum.*

67–68. *Triple tomoe motif with* miru *motif. Decorated writing* ▷
paper for the "Minori" chapter of the Genji Monogatari *scrolls;*
Heian period, national treasure. Gotō Art Museum, Tokyo. On the
right is a picture of living mistletoe, on which the miru *motif may*
have been based.

and melons; *hōsōge karakusa*, peony *karakusa*, and chrysanthemum *karakusa*; lion medallions, phoenix medallions; running water, waves, and *sunagashi* (patterns of sprinkled gold and silver dust); interlocking circles, *kikkō* lattice, diamond shapes, and *suminagashi* (marbled effect produced by dropping ink on moistened paper). Of all these motifs, none expresses the special quality of the period better than the last mentioned; the *suminagashi* creates a beautiful effect of an image spreading freely over the paper through the unbounded flow of water.

The practice of dedicating to a temple an ornamented sutra was popular among the Heian aristocrats, but among many such productions none can equal in quality of design or skill of workmanship the thirty-three sutra scrolls presented in 1164 by Taira no

Kiyomori (1118–81) to his family shrine at Miyajima. The scrolls are now known as the Taira Dedicatory Sutras. Each of the scrolls is ornamented with metal and crystal fittings. The openwork metal bands protecting the narrow edge of the scrolls are worked in fluid lotus *karakusa* and other designs. The covers sparkle with gold and silver leaf and sprinkled gold dust, against which appear clouds and mist, flowers and grasses, butterflies and birds, and other motifs full of the distinctive flavor of the Heian aesthetic at its fullest bloom. Polychrome ornament dazzles the eye with *kikkō hanabishi*, *hōsōge karakusa*, lotus *karakusa*, and various geometrical patterns. Among the designs on the backings of the scrolls can be found cloud and mist patterns shining in the shimmering light of sunset like the skies of Heaven (Plate 57), peonies in vases re-

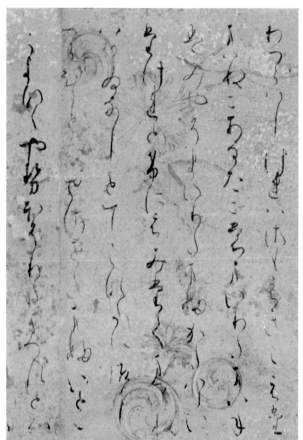

sembling the offeratory flowers on Buddhist altars, and lions among auspicious clouds. Each scroll opens with an illustration, comparable to a frontispiece, that is appropriate to the contents of the sutra inscribed therein. All the scrolls are truly remarkable in the freshness of overall conception and composition and the imagination displayed in the selection and execution of decoration.

It is surely no exaggeration to call the papers of the *Anthology of the Thirty-six Poetic Geniuses* and the Taira Dedicatory Sutras the most stunning collections of the decorative motifs of the late Heian period.

Motifs Originating in the Heian Period

On the decorated paper for the introductory text of

the "Minori" chapter of the *Genji Monogatari* is found a pattern of triple *tomoe* ("giant comma") and *miru* (a type of seaweed). This occurrence of the *tomoe* in a work dating from the first years of the twelfth century is its earliest appearance as a purely decorative motif (Plate 67–68). The patterns on clothing worn by figures in the Heian-period narrative scrolls offer ample illustration of popular motifs. The excited people in the *Ban Dainagon* scroll (Plates 69–70) wear outfits decorated with the *tomoe* and *kaede* (maple leaf) motifs. A court lady in the *Genji* scroll (Plate 72) wears a robe with a *kikkō* motif. The so-called *miru* motif can also be found on the costumes of peasants in the *Shigisan Engi* scroll (Plate 71) and on the lacquer and mother-of-pearl inlay saddle in the Tamukeyama Shrine in Nara Prefecture. In the latter example, however, the plant

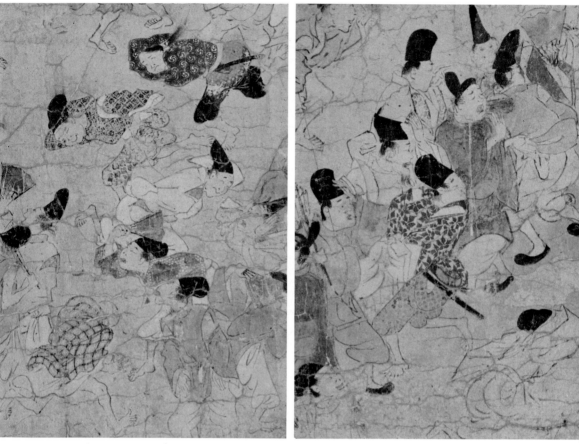

69–70. *Garments showing* tomoe *(left, top) and maple-leaf (right) motifs. Details from* Ban Dainagon Ekotoba *narrative scroll; Heian period, national treasure. Sakai Collection, Tokyo.*

may actually be mistletoe (Plate 67–68), and the motif on the saddle usually is referred to as the "mistletoe medallion" design.

Among other original Heian-period motifs, there is another type of medallion format known as *ban-e*, which was printed on cloth or paper with a carved wooden block. The most common motif used in this printing technique is the lion enclosed in a circle, although medallions with phoenixes, wisteria, or other motifs occur frequently in textile designs. Considered as a single motif, the *ban-e* belongs to the lineage of the phoenix medallion on the Chinese-style chest in the Hōryū-ji treasures. In the mid-Heian period, there occurred radical changes in the clothing styles of the aristocrats, and plain-colored twills came to be pre-

ferred over Chinese brocades. On these twills were often designs related to rank or to ceremonial occasions on which the outfit was to be worn.

The *karakusa* pattern was born out of the decorative arts related directly to Buddhism, and Buddhist arts were also responsible for popularizing the lotus pond motif. Outstanding examples of the lotus *karakusa* are found on an inlaid lacquer sutra case in the Nara National Museum (Plate 35) and on the cover of one of the Taira Dedicatory Sutras (Plate 65). Another fine specimen of the lotus-pond theme is to be found on the side of a sutra case dated 1175 in the Nanatsu-dera temple in Nagoya (Plate 73).

An overview of the design motifs popular during the Heian period reveals the early decades as a period

71. Miru *motif. Detail from* Shigisan Engi *scroll; Heian period, national treasure. Chōgonsonshi-ji, Nara.*

72. Kikkō *(tortoise shell) motif. Detail from "Yadorigi" section,* Genji Monogatari *scroll; Heian period, national treasure. Tokugawa Art Museum, Nagoya.*

73. *Lotus-pond motifs. Sides of stacked lacquer sutra boxes; Heian period (dated 1175), important cultural property. Nanatsudera, Aichi Prefecture.*

of transition, strongly reflecting the T'ang taste which had dominated Nara design. From mid-Heian onward, the prominence of the Jōdo sect resulted in the widespread construction of temples dedicated to Amida, with rich new modes of interior ornamentation. Among motifs, the imported *hōsōge* floral pattern predominated, but in it was incorporated an increasingly pronounced native flavor. As for other types of decorative motifs that originated during the Heian period, pictorial designs showing natural scenery and everyday occurrences, and the medallion motif—important later as the basis of family crests—also emerged. The *kirikane* technique developed a repertoire of geometric and floral shapes, which continued to be executed in other mediums after the *kirikane* technique declined. Inspired and nourished by the four hundred years during which there flourished a highly refined aristocratic culture dedicated to aesthetic cultivation, the motifs of this period exhibit a richness and warmth of sentiment that characterize the purely Japanese taste.

5

Increasing Severity

Kamakura Period (1185-1392)

At the end of the twelfth century, political power shifted from the aristocracy to military men, and though the court remained in Kyoto, the effective center of government was moved to Kamakura in the east. The cultural center of the country remained with the aristocrats in Kyoto, for their firmly rooted traditions could not be snatched from them even though their political influence could. On the contrary, as the new political-military leaders and their supporters entered a period of relative calm following the turbulence that surrounded the transferral of power, they tried to assume the traditional life style of the aristocracy with virtually no alterations. Therefore, to the extent that the cultural life of Kyoto underwent no drastic change, the old forms lived on in new guises. Certainly, this was true of decorative motifs: the patterns themselves did not change markedly, although their manner of expression came gradually to reflect the personalities of the new military patrons of the arts.

Motifs Taken from Nature

Bush clover blooms riotously, a family of deer rests momentarily on the bank of a swift-flowing stream, and small birds dart through the sky in the mellow autumn landscape that covers a small inlaid-lacquer box in the Izumo Shrine (Plate 74). In this decoration, the sentimentalism of Heian lacquer ware can still be sensed, but the individual forms, particularly the deer and birds, have become more naturalistic and ani-

74. Pictorial motif of deer and bush clover. Lacquer box with gold, silver, and mother-of-pearl inlay; Kamakura period, national treasure. Izumo Shrine, Shimane Prefecture.

mated. Replacing the feeling of nostalgia that characterized similar Heian designs is a new realism. Even in a design such as this can be detected the transformation from the refined and delicate tastes of the Heian nobility to the vital dynamism of the new military leaders. Another example is the mother-of-pearl inlaid-lacquer writing box, belonging to the Tsurugaoka Hachiman Shrine in Kamakura, on which appears a naturalistic representation of chrysanthemum clusters bordered by a woven bamboo fence. The choice of mother-of-pearl inlaid in a ground of gold filings heightens the cool intellectuality of the composition, and one cannot help but feel a certain severity underlying its subdued elegance—an identifying feature of Kamakura-period works of art.

A frequent theme in the painting and lacquer ware of the time is the scenery of Sumiyoshi, outside Osaka, and the religious observances honoring the Shinto deities of the Sumiyoshi Shrine. Also popular were scenes of Awaji-shima, the island near Kobe which is supposedly the site of the grave of Izanagi, one of the Shinto procreators of the universe. On a lacquer box in the Rinnō-ji temple in Nikko appears a classic treatment of the Awaji-shima motif. A *torii* gate to a shrine and pine trees stand within a *suhama* (stylized "sandbar") shape, plovers flying above the waves, Awaji-shima adrift on the open sea beneath the new moon; on the shore are fishing boats and a saltmaker's hut, and cranes among the rushes. The representation of this scene is detailed and naturalistic.

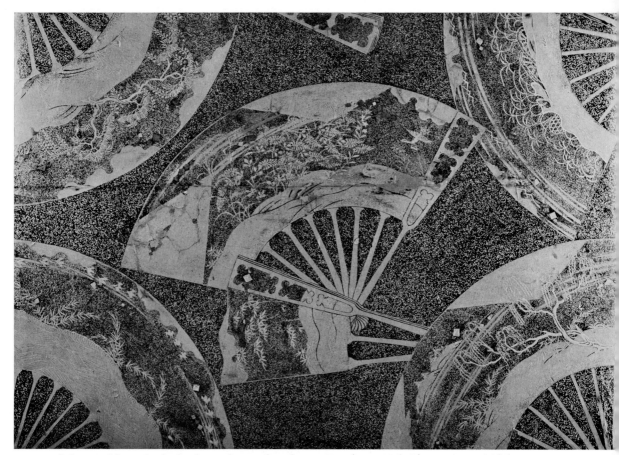

75. *Motif of scattered fans.* Chōshōden *lacquer box; surface of cover; Kamakura period. Okura Museum, Tokyo.*

76. *(Above) Butterfly motif. Inner surface of cover of inlaid lacquer* ▷ *box; Kamakura period, national treasure. Hatakeyama Museum, Tokyo.*

77. *Bamboo and sparrows motif. Reverse of a bronze mirror;* ▷ *Kamakura period. Dōmyō-ji Tenman-gū, Osaka.*

78. *Plum tree, cypress fence, and sparrows. Rubbing of mirror back;* ▷ *Kamakura period. Tokyo National Museum.*

79. *Motif of scattered fans.* Chōshōden *lacquer box; one side, showing metal fittings; Kamakura period. Okura Museum, Tokyo.*

The majority of such motifs drawn from nature are done in a style and technique identical to that of the *Yamato-e* tradition in painting. They emphasize seasonal detail and intimate atmosphere rather than a panoramic view. For instance, the reverse of the lid of the Chōshōden lacquer box in the Okura Museum (Plate 81) is surprisingly similar to the garden landscapes in the *Kasuga Gongen Reigenki Emaki* (scroll of the miraculous deeds of the Kasuga deity; dated 1309) in the Kasuga Shrine, Nara.

Intellectual Compositions

Patterns based upon intellectual arrangements of diverse elements are perhaps the most representative type of decorative motif from the Kamakura period. Exemplifying this type is the design of scattered fans on the *Chōshōden* lacquer box in the Okura Museum (Plates 75 and 79). On the open faces of the fans scattered across the surface of the box are lovely scenes of the four seasons. Seven fans ornament the cover: five are fully open, one partially open, and one folded tightly. On each side of the box are two open fans and one folded one. Even the gilt metal fittings repeat the shape of the fans in the formal conception of the composition. Heian-period designs were largely emotional or symbolic in content, but this one is entirely rational and "intellectual." Similar lacquer boxes with fan decorations were also made during the Muromachi period, but by that time the arrangements had become

80. Peony karakusa with butterfly motif. The magnificent gold, silver, and mother-of-pearl inlaid ornamentation of this lacquer box forms a composition that is at once lyrical and rational. The medallions on the butterfly wings show a variety of motifs popular at the time. Kamakura period; national treasure. Hatakeyama Museum, Tokyo.

81. Ashide *pattern. Chōshōden lacquer box; inner surface of cover; Kamakura period. Okura Museum, Tokyo.*

82. *Black-lacquer ornamented saddles with mother-of-pearl inlay. Left: cherry-tree motif; Kamakura period, important cultural property. Tokyo National Museum (formerly Asano Collection). Right: Ashide motif in a design of rocks and branches; Kamakura period, national treasure. Eisei Bunko Archives.* ▷

more random and distinctly less formal than the Kamakura prototypes. The folding fan motif also appeared on other objects of the Kamakura period, including mirror backs and armor.

Other designs in this category are chrysanthemums within a *suhama* framework, as on the lacquer box in the Tokyo Hatakeyama Museum (Plates 84–85); the cypress-fan medallions and *suhama* lacquer box in the Tokyo National Museum; and the *suhama*-and-plovers lacquer box in the Nomura Collection. An entry dated 1185 in the *Sankaiki*, the diary of a court minister, mentions an inlaid lacquer chest decorated with *suhama* and plovers showing that this combination of motifs was already in use by the end of the Heian period. The *suhama* motif was used with increasing frequency throughout the Kamakura period. Its purely

formal and decorative shape appealed strongly to the Japanese sense of pattern.

Arrangements of peonies with butterflies were already known during the Heian period, and the poetic theme of butterflies hovering above blossoms may well be understood as an expression of Japanese sensibilities regarding nature. But the peony and butterfly pattern adorning the lacquer box in the Hatakeyama Museum (Plate 80) differs markedly from its predecessors. The butterflies are intermingled with a *karakusa* pattern of outsized peonies in a manner which is neither naturalistic nor simply random: a definite logic underlies the powerful composition. The pattern is essentially an idealization of reality. Above and beyond the sweetness of the motif, the decoration of the box combines the distinctive beauties of three separate techniques of

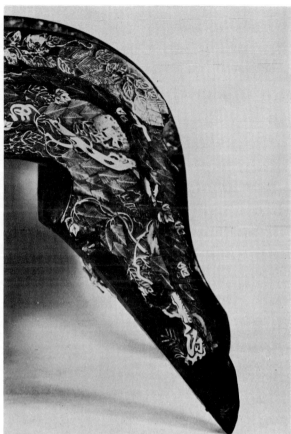

lacquer decoration: gold inlay, silver-sheet application, and inlaid mother-of-pearl. The result is a magnificent creation of great beauty and superb elegance.

Ashide Patterns

The so-called *ashide* ("reed calligraphy") pattern originated as illustrations in which ornately written decorative ideograms were inserted in pictures of reeds and water, such as frequently appeared on the decorated papers used for inscribing poetry. Eventually, even in pictures which did not represent reeds and water, the inclusion of ideograms in the design kept the name *ashide*. An alternative name for such illustrations is *uta-e* ("poem pictures"), a term which was already in use during the Heian period, and occurs in both the

Genji Monogatari and the *Eiga Monogatari*. The classic example is in the Taira Dedicatory Sutras: ideograms meaning "sutra" are incorporated into the design on the cover, and elsewhere ideograms appear ornamentally on the writing paper of the scrolls. Carrying this device on from the earlier period, Kamakura designers made extensive use of themes including special ideograms from Chinese poetry. On a lacquer box belonging to the Mishima Shrine, a single panel screen stands beneath a blossoming plum tree while water fowl swim in a pond and a flock of wild geese wing their way across the gardenlike landscape. Scattered among these motifs are the ideograms for "brocade," "curtain," "wild goose," "prosperity," "tradition," and "journey," all taken from a famous poem by the T'ang poet Po Chü'i (772–846) on which the scene is based.

83. Scattered grasses and flowers. The decoration of the inner surface of the cover of a lacquer cosmetic box continues the tradition of Plate 66. The variety of plants is greater, however, and they are rendered in more naturalistic fashion, reflecting a marked change in attitudes toward ornamentation. Kamakura period; national treasure. Suntory Museum, Tokyo.

84–85. Chrysanthemums in a suhama pattern (detail of cover and ▷ full view). A suhama (stylized "sandbar" form) fills the center of each side of this lacquer box, while quarter-shapes are placed at each corner. The suhama enclose sprays of chrysanthemums scattered at random but falling into a loose, informal symmetry. Chrysanthemums were a favorite decorative motif from the Kamakura period onward, and this box is a superb example of an early version of the motif. Kamakura period. Hatakeyama Museum, Tokyo.

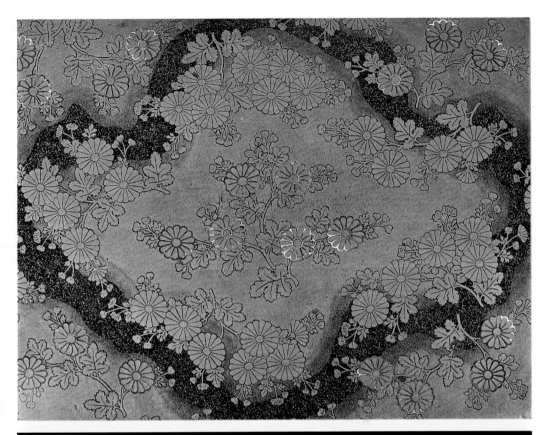

86. Butterfly, chrysanthemum, and running water motifs. Detail and full view of a carved metal arm guard; Kamakura period, national treasure. Kasuga Shrine, Nara.

The *Chōshōden* lacquer box mentioned above, with the exterior decoration of scattered fans, has a design of plum and willow trees on the inner surface of the lid (Plate 81); arranged below the trees are the first five characters of the poem from which the box takes its name. These are the first few lines of the poem, contained in the eleventh-century anthology, *Wakan Rōeishū*:

> The seasons linger in the Palace of Eternal Life
>   (*Chōshōden*)
> Before the Gate of Lasting Youth, both sun and
>   moon stand still.

The Chōshōden (Chinese: *Ch'ang-shen-tien*) was a hall in the Hua Ching Kung, a T'ang palace, usually reserved as the emperor's private residence. This parti-

cular poem is a congratulatory one and wishes long life to the emperor. As such, it was a favorite theme in various Japanese arts.

In their treatment of themes from Chinese or Japanese poems, the two lacquer boxes just mentioned are representative of the special taste of the Kamakura period. Equally representative is an ornate saddle, inlaid with mother-of-pearl, in the Eisei Archives (Plate 82, right). The decoration is based upon a poem by the monk Jien (?1155–1255) in the *Shin Kokinshū* anthology:

> Our love no deeper than the dye
>   of autumn rains in the pines,
> Dispelled by winds that sweep across
>   Makuzugahara

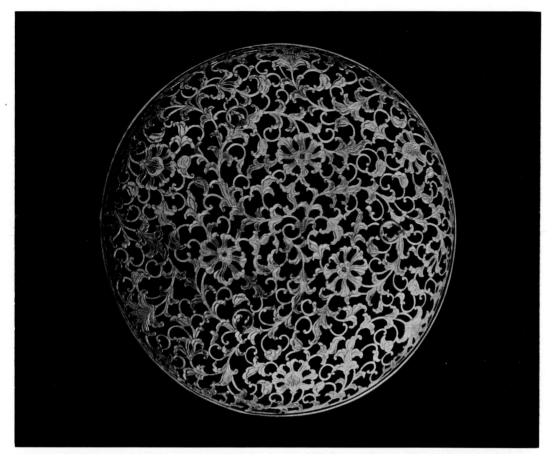

87. Peony karakusa *motif. Openwork gilt-bronze basket for use in Buddhist rituals; Kamakura period, national treasure. Jinshō-ji, Shiga Prefecture.*

In the complex surface decoration of the saddle, pine trees drenched by late autumn rain are combined with ideograms from the poem. A surprisingly airy effect has been obtained even with such rigid material as mother-of-pearl.

Other patterns which illustrate particular poems without actually incorporating ideograms in the design are encountered frequently in works of this period; during the succeeding Muromachi period, such motifs were to flourish under the name *uta-e,* among which are to be found numerous masterpieces.

Other Kamakura Motifs

Among the floral motifs found on Kamakura-period works of art are cherry trees and blossoms (as on the mother-of-pearl inlaid-lacquer saddle; Plate 82, left), peony *karakusa* (as on the ritual flower basket in the Jinshō-ji temple, Shiga Prefecture; Plate 87), and chrysanthemums with butterflies and waves (as on the arm guard in the Kasuga Shrine, Nara; Plate 86). Among animal motifs are to be found dragons, lions, and tigers prowling amid bamboo. Among medallion motifs may be listed the design of butterfly wings and *tomoe,* interlocking circles, *kuyō* designs of nine circles based on astrological symbols, whirlpool patterns, chrysanthemums, plum blossoms, and cartwheel designs. As can be seen from this partial listing, the search by craftsmen and artists for new motifs continued to extend out to ever-widening sources of themes.

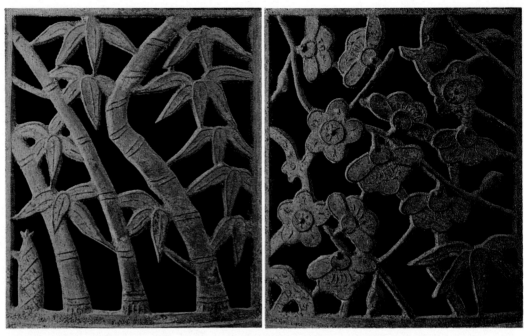

88. Plum blossom and bamboo motifs. Although the green patina on these six-paneled bronze lanterns gives the object a certain beauty, the composition of each panel and the arrangement of the separate motifs is even more impressive. Muromachi period; important cultural property. Tokyo National Museum.

89. Snow-laden willow motif. Heavy snow bends downward the branches of an old willow in a popular pattern that is rendered here in karaori *weave on a* Nō *costume. Momoyama period. Tokyo National Museum.*

6

Influence of Yüan and Ming Styles
Muromachi Period (1392-1568)

After the introduction of Zen to Japan during the Kamakura period, Japanese monks traveled regularly to China for religious studies, and returned with art objects from the continent. Later, with the establishment of trade relations with China during the Muromachi period, the flow of such items into Japan increased somewhat. But it was never large, and the Chinese objects found their way quickly into the hands of the small number of aristocrats. Treasured only in temples or the residences of the elite, the Yüan and Ming Chinese decorative styles reflected in these objects were not available to the majority of ordinary Japanese. Native artisans therefore had little opportunity to see foreign motifs and little incentive to learn the Chinese techniques of, for example, carved lacquer or brocade. Few such objects were made in Ja-

pan, and the demand for luxury goods was satisfied, for the most part, by trade with Ming China.

And yet, the influence of Yüan and Ming styles and designs gradually became apparent in the handicrafts of Muromachi Japan. This development was particularly pronounced during the so-called Higashiyama era in the mid-sixteenth century when Yoshimasa, the eighth Ashikaga shogun, encouraged the imitation of Chinese styles by Japanese craftsmen. The period takes its name from the hilly eastern section of Kyoto where the shogun and his retainers built their villas. The first revelation of Chinese influence during this period came in decorative motifs; only later did actual innovations of form or techniques of manufacture follow.

Chinese influence in the decorative arts was particularly apparent in lacquer ware. The type of carved cin-

90. Camellia motif. Carved lacquer portable case for books and sutras; Muromachi period. Kanagawa Prefectural Museum, Yokohama.

nabar lacquer ware known generally as *Kamakura-bori* (Kamakura carving) actually originated in China. Among the popular decorative motifs on this ware are many which were borrowed directly from imported Chinese pieces; others show skillful adaptation of native motifs such as the camellia (Plate 90), chrysanthemum, crane, and tortoise. Another type of lacquer ware, inlaid with gold, called *chinkin* (sunken gold) was also based on Chinese models, both in techniques of manufacture and in the use of Chinese decorative themes combined with Japanese.

Lacquer ware reflected most clearly the influence of Chinese styles on the decorative arts of the Muromachi period, but Chinese themes and techniques appeared also in painting and other arts. The tea ceremony, which originated in China, attained its full develop-

ment in Japan during the fifteenth and sixteenth centuries, taking on an increasingly Japanese aesthetic taste in the varied arts that it spawned. The making of heavy iron kettles for use in the tea ceremony involved Chinese techniques, and the range of motifs used in decorating the kettles was wide: along with traditional landscapes and flora, there were novel Chinese subjects such as horses (Plate 97) and monkeys.

Ashide and Uta-e Patterns

The so-called *ashide* device of incorporating ideograms in the ornamental design, used frequently during the Kamakura period, continued to be popular in the Muromachi period, particularly in decorating *maki-e* inlaid lacquer. A representative example of the

91. Hut and human figure (ashide pattern). Inlaid lacquer writing box (inner surface of cover); Muromachi period, important cultural property. Nezu Art Museum, Tokyo.

later style is a famous lacquer writing box, now in the Kyoto National Museum, which takes its theme from the following poem in the *Kokinshū* anthology:

> Plovers perching on the rocks
> That jut out into the river
> Beneath Mt. Shio, cry
> "Thou, my lord, shall live forever!"

Chinese characters from the poem are incorporated into the design on the cover of the box. A box in the Tokyo National Museum decorated with a design based on the same poem shows two ideograms projecting above the rushing stream.

The famous writing box showing Mount Kasuga (Plate 91), which is thought to have been a favorite of the eighth Ashikaga shogun Yoshimasa, depicts the following poem by Mibu no Tadamine, also in the *Kokinshū*:

> Living in a mountain village,
> I feel loneliest in autumn,
> Awakened oftentimes at night
> By the deer's plaintive call.

Another writing box, in the Tokyo National Museum, illustrates the poem by Kuga no Dajō Daijin in the *Gosenshū* imperial anthology of 1251:

> Be it there,
> Through all eternity
> Atop Mt. Otokoyama
> The radiating moonlight
> I behold at the ridge.

92–93. Wild cherry motif. Inner surfaces of inlaid lacquer writing box illustrated in Plate 94; Muromachi period. Tokyo National Museum.

The landscape decoration of all these boxes shows strong Chinese influence, and such motifs seem to have been extremely popular, for many examples of their use on *maki-e* lacquer ware remain. As mentioned in the previous chapter, in *ashide* decoration the entire poem is never shown. Rather, a few key ideograms were selected from the poem and carefully fitted into the composition both to complement the design and to enhance its meaning. Together, ideograms and landscape formed a unified decorative expression of a type unique to Japan.

The related technique of *uta-e* (poem-picture) illustrated the significance or spirit of a poem without actually incorporating words in the design. It may seem contradictory that Japanese poetry should have been used to illustrate lacquer ware of a period that was so pervaded by reverence for the imported culture of Yüan and Ming China. But the wealthy Japanese connoisseurs of lacquer and other arts, despite their intense interest in China, were also well versed in the traditional Japanese arts; perhaps direct contact with a foreign culture made them even more strongly aware of their own traditions. In any case, the Muromachi period was a time in which Japanese poetry made itself felt not only in design motifs but in almost every aspect of the arts.

Sung and Yüan Styles in Lacquer

Naturalistic patterns formed the mainstream of Muromachi decorative style. Among the eleven lacquer boxes in the collection of the Kumano Hayatama

94. Branch of flowering wild cherry. Inlaid lacquer writing box (surface of cover); Muromachi period. Tokyo National Museum.

Shrine in Wakayama Prefecture, six are decorated with designs based variously on paulownia, oak, maple, peony, mandarin orange, and chrysanthemum. Generally, in the *Yamato-e* tradition of loving detail, the designs show a lone tree trunk or a single flowering stalk growing from the ground against a background of rocks or running water. But in the treatment of the trunks and branches or the rocks and streams there is a strong flavor reminiscent of Sung and Yüan painting styles. The lacquer writing box in the Tokyo National Museum, decorated with a wild cherry motif, is a good example (Plates 92–93 and 94). The strongest statement of the motif is on the cover of the box, where an entire branch of flowering cherry is shown; fragments of the motif reoccur on the inner surface of the lid and in the interior of the box. The blossoms, seen from

both front and back, are rendered in dull silver, while the twigs and leaves are done in gold inlaid in a ground of lacquer covered with gold dust. The total impression is one of refinement and subdued elegance. When the box cover is removed and turned over, a single sprig of the same cherry appears. Inside the box, in the separate sections for brushes and ink, cherry petals and whole blossoms lie scattered, as if by the wind. The water dropper shaped like a cherry blossom (Plate 92–93) is a later addition to the writing box. Although the box is a mere writing accessory, extraordinary care was obviously lavished on its decoration. Its design is intended to touch the emotions of the user and no doubt to put him in a special frame of mind whenever he sits down to write. It is designed to share in the life of its owner.

95. *Arrowroot* karakusa *motif. Section from the* Matsuhime Monogatari *scroll; Muromachi period (dated 1526). Tōyō University Collection, Tokyo.*

In illustrated narrative handscrolls, especially those of the Muromachi period, rules of proportion were frequently set aside by the artist in the interests of design or of intensifying the narrative content. A similar tendency is to be detected in the patterns ornamenting lacquer ware. The writing box with the Mt. Kasuga scene (Plate 91) is an excellent example of the craftsman's willingness to disregard naturalistic proportions. On the inner surface of the lid is a scene of a man reclining inside a small hut, listening to the distant cries of deer in the surrounding hills. Bush clover, pampas grass, and valerian are represented several times larger than the hut itself and bend over it more like trees than grass or flowers. The emphasis placed on the autumn vegetation intensifies the seasonal atmosphere, evoking the drowsy nostalgic mood of the poem illustrated (quoted above). This manner of subordinating naturalistic representation to the emotional content of what is otherwise a realistic scene is to be frequently detected in the arts of the Muromachi period.

Karakusa Patterns

Another interesting example of this playful distortion of perspective and proportion is to be seen in the *Matsuhime Monogatari* scroll (Plate 95), an illustrated fairy tale dated 1526. A hugely outsized *karakusa* vine twists its way through the section illustrated, dwarfing the small building and human figures. Dewdrops glitter on the leaves of this fantastic, totally imaginary

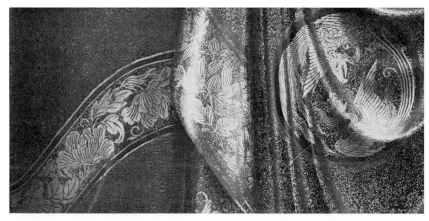

96. Phoenix medallion and peony karakusa. Lacquered wood statue of Shaka Nyorai; Muromachi period. Tokyo National Museum.

97. Horse motif. Ashiya-type kettle for tea ceremony; Muromachi period. Tokyo National Museum.

karakusa. As a motif, it belongs to the type of arrow-root *karakusa* which appears time and again in the textile pattern known as *tsujigahana* which developed during the latter half of the sixteenth century.

Among *karakusa* types, the classic honeysuckle, peony, and *hōsōge* versions continued to be widely used, but other common flowers also began to wind their way into *karakusa* motifs of Muromachi-period designs. These new flowers included plum, paulownia, wisteria, and chrysanthemum. Flowers were also added to the grape *karakusa* popular on Yüan and Ming underglaze blue porcelain, creating a *karakusa* type that is unique to Japan. Paulownia and chrysanthemum *kara-*

kusa appear on a number of the eleven lacquer boxes in the Kumano Hayatama Shrine. Plum *karakusa* decorates a set of lacquer writing box and lacquer writing table now in the Itsukushima Shrine.

The decorated objects described in this chapter have, for the most part, been lacquer ware, which was indeed one of the most distinguished of Muromachi-period arts. However, the tendency to welcome foreign motifs and apply them to decorative patterns was by no means restricted to lacquer. Such motifs appear also in textiles, in metal and wood crafts, in ceramics, and in all the other arts of the period.

7

Changing Taste
Momoyama Period (1568–1615)

The Momoyama period was a short but critical era in Japanese history. Lasting barely half a century, it was a time of political disunity and intense social chaos during which the established society collapsed and a new culture was born. Social, economic, and political transformations, which under calmer circumstances might well have required a full century or more, occurred with stunning speed.

In the world of design and decoration, the Momoyama period was a time of reconstruction. Many traditional themes were in decline or had already collapsed entirely. A complete rejection of tradition would not have been unnatural under such circumstances, but rather than rejection there occurred a reinterpretation of many classic motifs. In design, new life was breathed into the spirit of tradition.

Designs on Kōdai-ji Lacquer Ware

Among representative crafts of the Momoyama period is the group of gold- and silver-decorated lacquer ware known as *Kōdai-ji maki-e* (Kōdai-ji temple inlaid lacquer). The name derives from the fact that the pieces were created for use in the Kōdai-ji, the temple built in eastern Kyoto in 1605 by the widow of the warlord Toyotomi Hideyoshi and dedicated to the spirit of her husband. The lacquer decorations in the mausoleum of the temple and the various furnishings made for the temple, as well as other lacquer ware that subsequently adopted the distinctive style, are now known as Kōdai-ji lacquer.

In Hideyoshi's mausoleum, scattered motifs incorporating musical instruments decorate the altar, the

98. Autumn grasses motif. Inlaid lacquer chest for books of poetry; Momoyama period. Kōdai-ji, Kyoto.

balustrades, and pillars, while a pattern of water-borne blossoms ornaments the central staircase. The outer surfaces of the doors to the small shrine on the altar are resplendent with pampas grass and paulownia, while their inner surfaces are decorated with chrysanthemum, maple, and paulownia designs. All this gold and silver decoration is set into black lacquer, creating an effect of great luxury and sumptuousness. Perhaps the reason for this extraordinary extravagance is the fact that much of this decoration may not have been intended for use in the temple. An inscription on the inside of the altar doors records their completion in 1596, antedating the construction of the temple by nearly a decade. According to temple tradition, they were brought to the Kōdai-ji from Hideyoshi's castle at Azuchi when the temple was built, and the decora-

tion in the Kōdai-ji mausoleum was apparently identical to that of certain chambers in the now-destroyed Azuchi castle.

Among the lacquer pieces in the Kōdai-ji are certain household furnishings that Hideyoshi and his immediate family used daily. It is believed that Hideyoshi frequently dined off the *kakeban* (high-legged eating tray) decorated with a motif of rushes in the traditional pictorial manner. The stationery box (Plates 99 and 100), the chest for poem books (Plate 98), the lamp-stand (Plate 101), and other items gorgeously decorated with *akigusa* (autumn grasses) motifs are believed to have been treasured possessions of Hideyoshi's wife. The lacquer technique of these pieces is not particularly complicated, but the composition of the patterns is strong and refined and has a beauty that draws upon,

99. *Autumn-grasses and bamboo-grove motifs with "lightning bolt" division. Inlaid lacquer stationery box; Momoyama period. Kōdai-ji, Kyoto.*

but is not restricted by, the canons of tradition. In design as well as in technique, the Kōdai-ji lacquer pieces exhibit a style that is as fresh and inventive as it is sumptuous.

On the Kōdai-ji lacquer ware the predominant patterns represent the grasses and flowers of autumn, the *akigusa*: chrysanthemums, wild camomile, pampas grass, bush clover, Chinese balloon flowers, agueweed, gentians, fringed pinks, arrowroot, morning glories, valerians, and rose mallows. Other popular motifs include pine, bamboo, clouds and mist, flowers floating down a stream, musical instruments, and paulownia or chrysanthemum medallions. The familiar older animal motifs and *karakusa* patterns are almost nowhere to be found.

Akigusa motifs were considered particularly appropriate for decorating articles used by women. The treatment of the motif combines a relaxed, natural mood with skillful composition in an unpretentious manner. This treatment seems to have been derived from the *akigusa* motifs appearing on a set of ten painted cypress-wood fans of the Muromachi period that belong to the Kumano Hayatama Shrine in Wakayama Prefecture.

During the Momoyama period, as many great castles and palaces were being built, large wall surfaces became available to painters for decoration. Wall coverings, *fusuma* (paper-covered sliding doors), and standing screens were lavishly ornamented with colorful painting, their surfaces often covered with gold foil before being painted. Landscapes and motifs of blooming flowers or grasses were the favorite subjects, chosen with the purpose of bringing familiar scenes into the interior of a room. This new approach to deco-

100. Detail of autumn-grasses and bamboo-grove motifs on inlaid lacquer stationery box illustrated in Plate 99; Momoyama period. Kōdai-ji, Kyoto.

ration extended also to the innovation of decorating lacquer furnishings with harmonious patterns of *akigusa*.

Some Kōdai-ji lacquer pieces show the compositional device of dividing the ornamented area into uneven sections, separated by the *matsukawabishi* (pine-bark diamond) outline or a zigzag "lightning bolt" line and placing distinctly different patterns in each adjoining compartment. This device was used not only on lacquer, but also employed with dramatic success in kimono textiles and on pieces of ceramic ware. The device probably was derived from the practice already common during the Muromachi period of separating areas of decoration by a diagonal straight line. An outstanding example of the technique, as elaborated on the Kōdai-ji lacquers, is the stationery box with bamboo and *akigusa* motifs that belonged to Hideyoshi's

wife (Plates 99 and 100). A bamboo grove with young shoots springing up out of the earth is dramatically juxtaposed with a luxuriant pattern of blooming autumn plants, creating a thematic contrast of spring and autumn as well as a visual harmony of the straight lines of the bamboo and the curving, undulating lines of the flowers and grasses.

Another characteristic Momoyama design is the addition of crestlike medallions of stylized chrysanthemum or paulownia to naturalistic renderings of floral themes, establishing a subtle contrast of natural form and conceptual device (Plate 101). In Momoyama designs, pampas grass is almost always shown drenched with dew, strongly emphasizing the atmospheric quality of the composition. These innovations in themes and styles of composition carried over without alteration into the early Edo period, where they dominated

101. Autumn grasses and medallions of chrysanthemum and paulownia. Inlaid lacquer lantern cover; Momoyama period. Kōdai-ji, Kyoto.

the designs of the early decades of the seventeenth century.

Designs on Kosode and Nō Costumes

During the Muromachi period, the *kosode*, a kimono with short hanging sleeves which had theretofore been used only as an undergarment, began to be worn as an outer garment suitable for all but the most formal occasions. Momoyama *kosode* became, consequently, objects of the most magnificent textile designs. The wearing apparel of the aristocracy had long been distinguished by gorgeous colors and superb textile quality. Now textile designing became another vehicle for the genius of artists, as important as lacquer ware,

ceramics, metal working, and other handicrafts.

After the ravages of the Onin civil war (1467–77) had abated, fugitive Kyoto weavers began settling in the Nishijin area, which had been the campground of the western faction during the dispute. The textiles produced by the Nishijin weavers included *neriginu* or glossed silk, *habutae* resembling soft taffeta, and a type of plain-colored twill called *aya*. Throughout the Momoyama period, the Nishijin looms produced such vast quantities of these various silks that they came into the possession of even low-ranking soldiers and commoners. The elegant textiles provided the surface for an extraordinary variety of decorative techniques, including impressed metal foil, *shibori* (tie-dyeing), highly differentiated styles of embroidery, and painted

102. Lilies and imperial ox-carts on tatewaku *ground. Nō costume embroidered with gold and colored thread; Momoyama period. Tokyo National Museum.*

designs. Textiles decorated with combinations of these techniques were made into kimono whose simple shapes were perfect foils for the splendor of their ornamentation.

Toward the end of the Momoyama period, the invention in Japan of the dazzling brocade known as *kara-ori* (literally, "Chinese weaving," but despite the name, a native Japanese product) created a new type of material for use in costumes for women's roles in the Nō drama, replacing the gold and multicolored brocades that had previously been imported from Ming China. Only the richest materials were used in the making of *kara-ori* brocade and the patterns decorating the fabric were appropriately lavish.

Within the popular culture, various forms of dance,

theatrical performances, and festival entertainments flourished, and elaborate costumes became a necessity for both performers and audience. Fashion was the concern of all classes. Foremost arbiters of taste were the courtesans and other women of leisure whose society had developed during the years of political confusion at the end of the Muromachi period. As major subjects of genre painting, these women exemplify the bold, flamboyant, and glittering atmosphere of contemporary society.

Few examples of the elaborately dyed and woven textiles of the Momoyama period remain today. Those that do, primarily Nō costumes, are in remarkably good state of preservation, however. Another primary source of information on the types of clothing

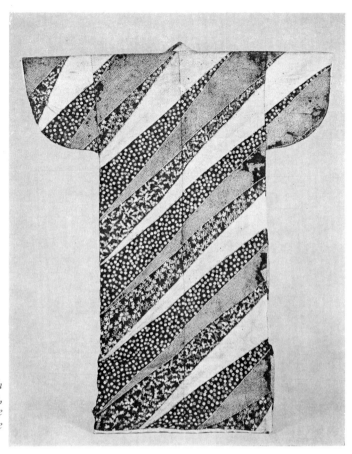

103–104. Temmon kosode *short-sleeved kimono with embroidered decoration of young pine, deer, and flowers, divided by sections of tie-dye patterns. A section of the same kimono is illustrated in close-up on the opposite page. Momoyama period. Tokyo National Museum.*

worn during Momoyama is the genre painting of screens and scrolls, in which artists reproduced with meticulous care the ornamentation of the garments worn at the time. Flowers, grasses, and trees associated with the four seasons stand out among the most popular motifs, and the *akigusa* and dew-drenched grasses also appear frequently. There are also many examples of motifs borrowed from earlier periods, including snow-laden willow branches (Plate 89) and water birds among rushes. The type of robe shown in Plate 103–104 usually goes by the name *Temmon kosode* (after the Temmon era, 1532–55), and was worn unbelted as a cloak over regular clothing for ceremonious occasions. This robe, in the Tokyo National Museum, is sectioned by acute-angle zigzagging lines of tightly worked *kanoko shibori* ("fawn spotted" tie-dyeing); in-

to the intervening spaces are fitted strikingly "modern" designs of maple and deer, young pine, and flowers rendered in embroidery. Another famous example of the elegant *Temmon kosode* is a robe with a *kikkō hanabishi* pattern (as in Plate 55) which once belonged to the wife of Hideyoshi and is now preserved in the Kōdai-ji.

Costume designs of earlier periods were revived during Momoyama, some of the most popular styles being the *kataginu*, an everyday article of clothing during the Heian period, and the *katami-gawari*, a kimono whose two sides were decorated with strikingly different patterns or colors. Many garments used gold leaf heavily: Nō robes with a gold geometric pattern or with motifs of grapes and poem cards worked in gold leaf on a purple ground combine simple tech-

105. Pampas grass and water birds. Embroidered silk textile; Momoyama period. Tokyo National Museum.

106. Snow-laden willow on fan shapes. Embroidered Nō costume; Momoyama period. Tokyo National Museum.

niques for a finished product of unsurpassed elegance. The Nō robe illustrated in Plate 102 has a light-brown ground of undulating vertical stripes worked in gold, on which are arranged towering lilies and small imperial carriages or ox-carts in a bold and ingenious manner.

Although its name is of unknown origin, the textile design called *tsujigahana* (crossed flowers) is inseparably associated with Momoyama taste (Plate 110). Designs featuring formalized chrysanthemums, wisteria, hollyhock, lotus, and cherry were created by a special technique of stitched tie-dyeing combined with delicately colored painted dyes and embroidery. The surface of the cloth is divided by a *matsukawabishi* (pine-bark diamond) silhouette which defines grounds of differing hues and distinct patterns. Nowhere does this bold de-

sign lapse into facile ornamentation. The predictable addition of dew to the leaves of the flowers and grasses expresses, like the lacquer patterns in the Kōdai-ji, some of the wistful sentimentality of the period.

Namban and Christian Designs

During the Momoyama period, trade flourished with Spanish and Portuguese merchants. Missionaries traveled along with the merchants, and for more than a half-century found Japan fertile ground for their proselytizing activities. A Christian church was built in Kyoto in 1577, and was popularly known as *Namban-ji* ("southern barbarian" temple). The term *namban* was applied indiscriminately to the odd-looking Europeans who arrived from the south and was used as an adjec-

107. Mugwort motif with chrysanthemum and paulownia crests. Embroidered kosode *kimono; Momoyama period. Matsuzakaya Textile Collection, Kyoto.*

108. Hydrangea and Chinese balloon-flower motif. Embroidered Nō costume; Momoyama period. Tokyo National Museum.

tive to describe anything concerned with them. Elements of European culture brought on Spanish or Portuguese ships were immediately seized upon by the curious Japanese as items of wonder and value. Within the realm of decorative motifs as well, *namban* themes enjoyed a great burst of popularity. Interest in foreign culture was not limited to clan leaders who made direct contact with the Europeans through trade or religion; even among commoners the fascination was great. The several *namban*-related motifs can be classified according to whether they are actually representations of odd-looking foreigners, Christian motifs, or designs based upon the various exotic customs of the Europeans as seen through Japanese eyes.

Motifs showing the foreigners themselves chiefly treat the arrival of the Spanish and Portuguese ships in Japanese ports. Typical is the lacquer chair in the collection of the Zuikō-ji in Kyoto, with its design of Portuguese nobles strolling with their dogs, surrounded by Western-style (nonfloral) *karakusa* and grapes, with an elephant cut-out (Plate 112–113). Other motifs of this type depict saddles and gunpowder flasks. The style is generally realistic, but the facial features and physiques of the unfamiliar Westerners tend to be rendered as caricatures.

Among motifs relating to Christianity should be listed utensils made in Japan for the celebration of the mass and household objects ornamented with crosses. For example, a reliquary in the possession of the Tōkei-ji temple in Kamakura has on its lid a cross and the IHS emblem of the Jesuit order, enclosed by a halo within a garland of Western-style *karakusa*.

109. Dew-drenched grass motif. Embroidered Nō costume; Momoyama period. Tokyo National Museum.

The exceedingly numerous third category of *namban* motifs, directly stimulated by the importation of foreign culture, might be described loosely as having a flavor of exoticism about them. A list of the subject matter would include firearms, European pipes, playing cards, European dogs, maps of the world, and Western-style *karakusa*. The delight in any new device and the skill with which such unfamiliar things were incorporated into Japanese design was remarkable. Among *namban* patterns, none is more representative of the spirit of the times than the above-mentioned *namban-karakusa*. The familiar Chinese winding-vine motif was combined with grapes or other Western fruit to give it an exotic touch. Such *namban* patterns maintained their popularity until the mid-Edo period. By then foreigners had been prohibited from entering Japan, Japanese Christians had been subjected to brutal persecutions, the popularity of European ideas and designs had passed, and *namban* had ceased to be part of the life of the Japanese.

Oribe Designs

Because the cultural relations established in earlier times with Ming China and Yi-dynasty Korea continued into the Momoyama period, a variety of crafts of continental origin also reached Japan. Together with objects that were imported, these provided tremendous stimuli to Japanese arts and crafts. Momoyama Japan was a nation vitalized by new technical capacities and enlarged sumptuary appetites, and production of woven textiles and ceramics expanded at an unprecedented

110. Cherry-blossom, wisteria, and ishi-datami *motifs, with "pine bark" division.* Tsujigahana *dyed textile; Momoyama period.*

rate. Although the various pottery kilns and pottery-making families drew heavily upon Korean techniques (even to the point of importing Korean potters), they also responded with sensitivity to the landscape peculiar to Japan and to the personality and tastes of the Japanese. During the Momoyama and Edo periods, the tea ceremony also provided a powerful force fostering the development of native forms and decorations.

The representative ceramic types of the Momoyama period were wares known as Shino and Oribe, both of which were produced in towns located in the Mino district north of Nagoya. These ceramics can be said to have resulted directly from the special conditions that prevailed during the Momoyama period. Technically, Shino and Oribe are virtually identical.

Oribe, however, is distinguished by having been produced according to the guidance and particular taste of the soldier and tea master Furuta Oribe. Most original Oribe pieces were made by the master potter Katō Kagenobu. The ware exhibits an independence of design and a range of patterns that are astounding in their variety and inspiration.

Generally, the motifs on Oribe ware fall into the following categories:

- *Motifs taken directly from life:* boats, folding fans, cartwheels, umbrellas, necklaces, rush curtains, combs, arrows, bridges, and eating utensils;
- *Geometrical motifs:* stripes, *kikkō* lattices, other lattices, diamonds, well-curb cross patterns, *tatewaku* or lozengelike patterns, wave patterns, fish-scale

111. Hydrangea on folding fans; clematis karakusa. *Embroidered Nō costume; Momoyama period. Tokyo National Museum.*

patterns, *ishi-datami* or paving-stone checkerboard, interlocking ring patterns, and circular rings;
•*Floral motifs:* plum, pampas grass, willow, chrysanthemum, Chinese balloon flower, lotus, melon, grape, bush clover, poppy, iris, and *karakusa;*
•*Other motifs:* landscapes and human figures.
Appearing on Oribe ceramics, these motifs are depicted in extremely straightforward patterns in an almost childlike manner. The composition on Oribe ware ranges from realistic representations to stylized abstract patterns and *karakusa,* often with several motifs combined in the *katami-gawari* (half-and-half) manner. Irregular stripe patterns, as in Plate 119, are often balanced by round, asymmetrical areas painted in contrasting colors. In the "half-and-half" compositions,

roughly one half of the surface is left plain while the other half is densely covered with varied patterns. This technique is related to similar devices used in weaving and *tsujigahana* dyeing. In compositions where many motifs are combined, the numerous versions include juxtaposition of floral and geometric motifs, patchwork joining of various patterns in arbitrary fashion, and intermingling of geometric and floral patterns in one continuous surface.

The categorization of Oribe motifs tends to belie the fact that they were selected from daily experience with such abandon and interpreted with such carefree independence that in many cases only the artist could tell what motif he had in mind. The patterns are generally abstract and impromptu, and mix various elements in-

112–113. Geometric motifs and Namban motifs. Left: Covered square ceramic dish, Oribe ware; Momoyama period. Suntory Art Museum, Tokyo. Right: Namban figures, Western-style karakusa with grapes, and elephant. Section of lacquer folding chair; Momoyama period. Zuikō-ji, Kyoto.

discriminately. But their peculiarly expressive power, strength of design, and subtle color combinations are unique to the Momoyama period. The patterns conform to the shape of the vessels they adorn, and the combination of solid, deep green glaze and iron oxide creates color harmonies of exceptional beauty. The decorative style of Oribe pottery had its parallels in other media, particularly weaving. Such parallels are not strict or direct, but are in the nature of a certain identity of taste. Perhaps the point is best made by saying that the Oribe plate illustrated in Plate 119 would look perfectly appropriate in the hands of a man

dressed in a kimono made of the fabrics of Plates 125 or 126.

The Momoyama period witnessed the introduction and proliferation of numerous new and exotic design motifs. At the same time, a modest renaissance was occurring in Japanese design, and classic pictorial and naturalistic motifs of the Heian period were revived and used extensively. This tendency, both conservative and innovative, increased in momentum late in the Momoyama period and grew more and more prevalent during the following Edo period.

8

Beginning of Modern Motifs

Edo Period (1615-1868)

The Edo period was a glorious age of crafts and fine arts. Following the unprecedented development of all the decorative arts, design motifs became increasingly varied and complex. Japan, as a small island country, has assimilated wave after wave of alien cultural influence willingly and quickly. Even so, if over a period of some two thousand years such a process has no outlet, it will inevitably create congestion, chaos, and confusion. Decorative motifs were no exception as they struggled to achieve innovation and novelty within a framework of tradition. Against a background of confusion, motifs of the Edo period seem to run wild in unrestricted proliferation. But Japan exhibited other tendencies appropriate to an island country. The feudal system at its peak of efficiency kept the country wholly at peace. The feudal government, headquartered in

Edo (present-day Tokyo), also imposed a strict policy of national seclusion, which kept the country free for more than two hundred years from new alien influences that would only have exacerbated the domestic confusion. Finally, the common people—particularly urban citizens with money but no official position—burst forth for the first time in Japanese history as the dominant cultural force in the society. The newly powerful urban, bourgeois culture fostered motifs that are unique to Edo and that grew directly out of their lusty, energetic way of life.

Although the Tokugawa shogunate established its headquarters in Edo, Kyoto continued to be the nominal capital of the land as well as the source and guardian of orthodox tradition and cultural taste. The cultural centers of Japan were thus divided both geographically

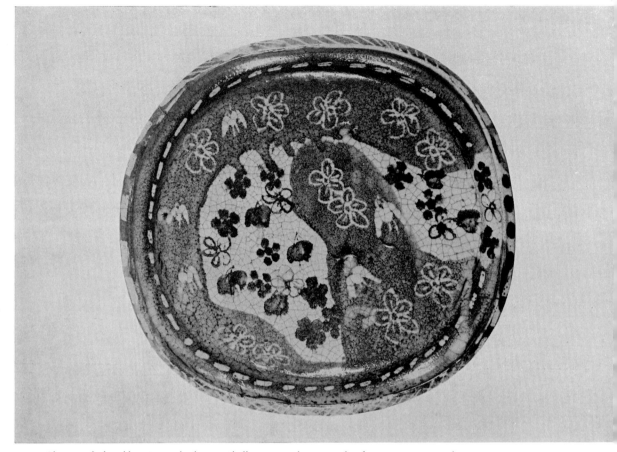

114. *Cherry and plum blossoms, with plovers. Shallow, gray Shino-ware bowl; Momoyama period.*

and socially. In contrast to Kyoto's conservatism, life in Edo and in other new merchant communities was progressive and occasionally flamboyant. Control of the economy had passed into the hands of the newly prosperous merchant class, and their financial backing gave a powerful incentive to the decorative arts. The same cultural influence was even more remarkable among the new bourgeoisie of Osaka and Sakai. The development of urban markets and the entertainment and prostitution districts that grew up around them awakened even the humblest classes of city dwellers and directed their attention toward the creation of new cultural conditions and decorative motifs that expressed their particular taste.

Another important aspect of Edo-period culture, the development of local clan governments, encouraged profitable regional industries. As a result, the various rural societies gave birth to new motifs of specifically regional flavor. The term *mingei* or "folk art" is given to those arts and crafts which emerged directly out of the needs of rural commoners and were of service to them in their daily lives.

Ornamentation of the Tōshōgū and Daiyūin Shrines

A clear and immediate impression of the character of one major stream of Edo-period decorative motifs is offered by the architectural decoration of the funerary shrines built at Nikkō for the Tokugawa shoguns. The Tōshōgū shrine was dedicated to the first shogun, Ieyasu, in 1636; and the Daiyūin was dedicated to the

115–118. Sword guards. Clockwise from top left: New moon, drenched grasses, and karakusa motifs; Edo period. Crab motif; Momoyama period. Tokyo National Museum. Crane-medallion motif; Momoyama period. Cherry blossom and fern motifs; Edo period. Kurokawa Bunka Kenkyūjo.

third shogun, Iemitsu, in 1653. Both shrines have been criticized for their "un-Japanese" ornateness, but as a sort of encyclopedia of design for the period, they incorporate every variety of motif and handicraft technique of common use in Japan from the Nara period to the Edo. Moreover, in such features as pillars ornamented with a chestnut pattern, they display skillful adaptations of Ming Chinese patterns.

Sword Guards

From the Muromachi period through the Edo period, one object that particularly benefited from innovations in design and decoration was the *tsuba* or sword guard. The *tsuba* is the metal fitting on a sword that protects the wielder's hand, separating the blade from the part of the sword held by the hand. From the late Momoyama period, *tsuba* began to be appreciated as vehicles for creativity of design and as works of art, valued for their appearance as much as for their function. Perhaps the long peace of the Edo period and the fact that swords were more important as symbols of status than as weapons of warfare contributed to the greater consideration paid to their decoration. At any rate, remarkable ingenuity and superb craftsmanship were lavished on the design of post-Momoyama sword guards. Some idea of the beauty and variety of *tsuba* will be gained from those illustrated in Plate 115–118.

Designs of the Kōrin School

Among individual artists who developed uniquely

119. Stripe pattern. Few other types of traditional Japanese ceramics have the peculiarly modern quality of Oribe ware. This square plate combines the characteristic Oribe green glaze with vertical stripes in brown iron oxide. On the beige ground the stripes are plain and regular; on the white ground they are thick and thin in the so-called mother and child manner. Momoyama period. Nezu Museum, Tokyo.

120. Pictorial landscape design. This rather complicated landscape is rendered on a summer kimono of hemp cloth ▷ in the chayatsuji *technique of dyeing. The design offers a fine bird's-eye view, almost as though one were looking into a miniature garden. Sparing touches of embroidery interrupt the monochrome indigo design. Edo period. Daihiko Textile Research Institute, Tokyo.*

121. Ashide *motif. Lacquer and silver writing box with design of pontoon bridge and poem from the* Gosenshū Anthology; *designed by Hon'ami Kōetsu. Edo period, national treasure. Tokyo National Museum.*

122. Eight-plank bridge motif, with irises. Lacquer writing box with theme drawn from the Ise Monogatari; *designed by Ogata Kōrin. Edo period, national treasure. Tokyo National Museum.*

beautiful decorative motifs were the giants of the early Edo period, Tawaraya Sōtatsu (dates uncertain), Hon'ami Kōetsu (1558–1637), and Ogata Kōrin (1658–1716). Amid the decades of feverish activity that characterize the first century of the Edo period, these three men were able to define and maintain styles that were as personal as they were traditional and that had strong influence upon the decorative arts of later Edo artists. Kōrin, as inheritor of the styles of Sōtatsu and Kōetsu (who was Kōrin's great-grand-uncle), brought to maturity a fresh tradition of painting that came to be known as *Rimpa* or "Kōrin school." While distinguished by its freshness and innovative freedom of design, the *Rimpa* style was a direct and conscious outgrowth of the *Yamato-e* style that traced its sources back to the Heian period. Alongside their achieve-

ments in painting, all three men were masters of related decorative arts and are equally well known for their ceramics, lacquer designs, calligraphy, and book designs. A few of their best-known works, exhibiting the wide variety of their talents, are decorated writing papers and long poetry handscrolls with underpainting by Sōtatsu and supremely beautiful calligraphy by Kōetsu; the numerous tea-ceremony bowls produced by Kōetsu and treasured by tea masters; the paintings by Kōrin on ceramics from the hand of his brother Kenzan, himself a master potter; and lacquer-ware masterpieces such as Kōetsu's *Funabashi* ("boat bridge") writing box (Plate 121), and Kōrin's beautiful *Yatsuhashi* writing box decorated with the poetic theme of an eight-plank bridge crossing an iris pond (Plate 122).

123. *Striped design. Nō costume with striped patterns of contrasting thicknesses and colors; Edo period. Tokugawa Art Museum, Nagoya.*

124. *Lattice and* kikkō hanabishi *motifs. Stiff brocade Nō costume; Edo period. Tokugawa Art Museum, Nagoya.*

Costumes for Nō and Kyōgen

In the mid-Edo period, designs and techniques used formerly in the making of *kosode* were added to the repertoire of techniques of weaving brocade for Nō costumes. Departing from the formal ceremoniousness of the earlier Nō robes, the *kosode*-like designs on the Edo costumes tended toward a more contemporary elegance and refinement (Plates 123, 124, 125, 129, 130).

The patterns used to decorate Kyōgen costumes generally tended to reflect the lighthearted satire and humor of that form of popular drama. The designs were often ingenious and strikingly original, but never was beauty of design sacrificed for the striking effect of an odd or curious subject. On the *kataginu* (a stiffly starched, sleeveless robe), in particular, appeared such unexpected motifs as dried sardines, pine cones (Plate 132), or three-legged trivets (Plate 131). The motifs drew freely upon objects familiar in daily life, and in their bold arrangements reflected the forthright personality of the common people.

Kasuri

During the Edo period, nearly every region in Japan produced its own distinctive cotton fabric called *kasuri*. *Kasuri* is a form of patterned textile the design of which is produced by weaving specially dyed warp and woof threads. The technique of using such pre-dyed threads originated in India and reached Japan by way of Indonesia, the Philippines, and Okinawa. Among the various types of *kasuri*, perhaps that most commonly worn

125. *Lattice textile pattern. This pattern for a Nō cos-tume is also called "lattice stripe" when considered to be primarily a vertical stripe with a less prominent hori-zontal stripe. Although the design seems very simple at first glance, the subtle color relationships and the spacing and alternation of thick and thin lines should not be over-looked. Edo period. Tokyo National Museum.*

126. *Vertical stripe pattern. Textiles with vertical stripes were imported in quantity from southern China and southeast Asia during the Momoyama period. Having gained great popularity among common people, they were produced in Japan as well. Edo period. Tokyo National Museum.*

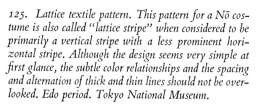

127. *(Above) Water and water plantain. The water design on this lacquer eating tray is stylized in taut folding* ▷ *lines; the water plantain are schematically represented to contrast with the supple lines of dew-laden pampas grass. Edo period. Tokyo National Museum.*

128. *Flower basket. Decorative nailhead cover. This charming basket heaped with lilies and Chinese balloon* ▷ *flowers worked in gold, silver, and cloisonné serves the plebian function of covering an unsightly nailhead. Edo period. Maeda Foundation, Tokyo.*

129. *Striped design with fine lattice. Nō costume; Edo period. Tokugawa Art Museum, Nagoya.*

130. *Lattice, Genji wheel, and lightning motifs. Stiff brocade Nō costume; Edo period. Tokugawa Art Museum, Nagoya.*

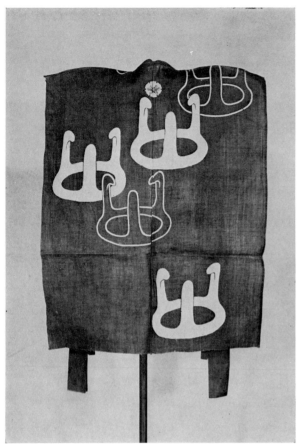

131. *Three-legged trivet motif.* Kataginu *jacket for* kyōgen *costume; Edo period.*

132. *Pine cone motif.* Kataginu *jacket for* kyōgen *costume; Edo period.*

(even in the twentieth century) was *kon-gasuri*, distinguished by its white patterns on a dark blue ground.

The special beauty of *kasuri* comes from the soft gradations of blue and white and from the gently blurred outlines of the patterns, both qualities resulting from weaving technique. Geometric patterns predominate, the most common being the familiar well-curb crosses, plain crosses, or crosses enclosed in *kikkō* lattice. Other varieties of *kasuri* incorporate pictorial designs in their decoration; look at the mouse motif and the pine and bamboo motif in Plate 133–134, the peony and lion motif in Plate 135, and the curious motif combining an auspicious hairy tortoise (a longevity symbol) with the ideogram *kotobuki* (long life, good fortune) in Plate 136. Purely pictorial motifs are fairly

rare, however, and are almost always used in combination with geometric patterns. On all *kasuri* the designs are vibrant and powerful, with a warmth emerging from their close connection with everyday life.

Stencil-dyed Textiles

As cotton fabrics began to be produced in large quantities, the technique of decorating them by stencil-dyeing gained prevalence. Stencils were made from tough handmade paper pasted together in several layers and treated with astringent persimmon juice to strengthen it. Dye-resistant rice paste was applied to the fabric through the cuts in the stencil and the fabric was dipped in dye. When the rice paste and surplus dye

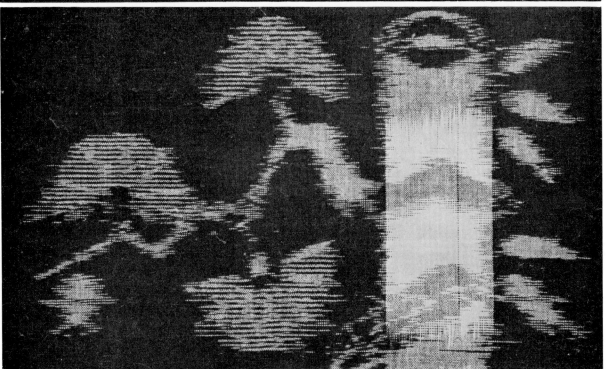

133–134. Kasuri. *Top: Mouse and flaming jewel. Bottom: Pine and bamboo motifs. Edo or Meiji periods. Tokyo National Museum.*

135. *Tree peony and Chinese lion motifs.* Kasuri *textile; Edo or Meiji periods. Tokyo National Museum.*

136. Kotobuki *(ideogram for longevity and good fortune) and long-tailed tortoise motifs.* Kasuri *textile; Edo or Meiji periods. Tokyo National Museum.*

137. *Stencil-dyeing patterns; Edo and Meiji periods. Left, top to* ▷ *bottom:* tatewaku *motif, geometric pattern, geometric pattern. Right, top to bottom:* kikkō *lattice enclosing crane medallion, carp ascending waterfall and Yajirobei figure, Genji wheel.*

were rinsed out of the fabric, white undyed areas identical to the cutout areas of the original stencil remained. As pure design, the stencil patterns were skillful and highly varied (Plates 137, 138). As a printing process, stencil-dyeing could be adapted to large-scale production, unlike the more painstaking hand-dyeing processes. This fairly simple stencil technique made for an extraordinary variety of patterns. Large, bold designs could be done as easily as small, highly intricate ones. Of the latter type, the so-called *Edo-komon* (small-figured designs) and the *bingata* textiles of the Ryūkyū Islands are the most outstanding.

Auspicious Symbols

The enchanted island of Taoist mythology, known as Hōrai-san in Japanese (P'eng-lai Shan in Chinese) was introduced from China early in Japanese history, and as a theme for decorative motifs went through a number of transformations. During the Heian period it was combined with the auspicious symbols of crane, tortoise, and pine; during the Kamakura period, the plum was added, and in Muromachi times, the bamboo. During the Edo period, the popular motif was simplified again, and was pared down to various combinations of pine-plum-bamboo or tortoise and crane appearing together with the three trees as symbols of good fortune. Another variation was the crane flying through the air with a branch of pine in its beak. These motifs appear on a great variety of clothing, household furnishings, and objects for special use on ceremonial occasions.

◁ *138. Stencil-dyeing patterns; Edo and Meiji periods. Left, top to bottom: wavy lattice, pine-bark lattice, irregular pine-bark pattern. Right, top to bottom: stylized iris pattern, maple leaves and autumn grasses in pine-bark areas,* miru *seaweed medallions.*

139. Boatman with rice bales. Section of a lacquer eating tray; Edo period. Tokyo National Museum.

Motifs Taken from Daily Life

As suggested earlier, the popular designs of the Edo period grew increasingly uninhibited in their sources of motifs. For subject matter, craftsmen and artists turned more and more to the objects of everyday experience, and the relationship between such objects and the lives of their users. Among the curiously plebian motifs that found their way into decoration were such things as vegetables, fish and shellfish, insect cages, paper umbrellas, large drums, powder puffs, bridges, carpenters' tools, and the like. Similarly, it was common to incorporate various occupations into decorative designs. Such activities as rice planting, hauling stones, pulling boats, hitching ox-carts, festival dancing—none of which had ever been considered dignified enough to serve as a decorative pattern—entered the realm of decoration during the Edo period.

These motifs found their way onto the clothing and utensils used daily in the lives of commoner artisans and merchants. On eating utensils in particular, a great variety of simple but effective designs made their appearance. Characteristic of such objects used for common purposes are the decorated lacquer eating trays in Plates 127 and 139, and the small metal plaque designed to cover the unsightly view of a nailhead on an interior beam (Plate 128).

Combined Animal and Plant Motifs

The transformations and developments of pattern designs reveal something of the changing tastes of each

140. *Insect cages in landscape motif.* Chayatsuji *textile; Edo period.*

succeeding generation. Over the course of the history of Japanese design, certain motifs were born or were borrowed, were developed and elaborated upon, and were combined with other motifs to form countless variations and proliferations. Motifs created for religious or aristocratic use during earlier periods were adapted for popular use during the Edo period. The Nara butterfly and peony motif reappeared as a popular Edo motif as did the Kamakura bamboo and tigers, bamboo and sparrows, and peonies with lions motifs. Other plant-and-animal combined motifs that gained wide popularity in the Edo period included squirrels with grapes and nightingales amid plum blossoms. Other new animal motifs included the rabbit in the moon, mice pulling rice cakes, and carp fighting their way up waterfalls (Plate 137, center right).

Picture-frame Composition

During the Edo period, there arose the technique of placing designs in a frame of a distinctive pattern, which was itself comprised of certain design motifs such as paper fans or poetry cards. In many cases these outline shapes bore no relation to the design they enclosed; in others they were combined with complementary motifs. The technique was most popular in decorating clothing and household utensils, and was also widely used on interior architectural fittings such as transoms, windows, and sliding paper doors.

Shapes of Objects as Decorative Forms

Within the realm of traditional handicrafts, there

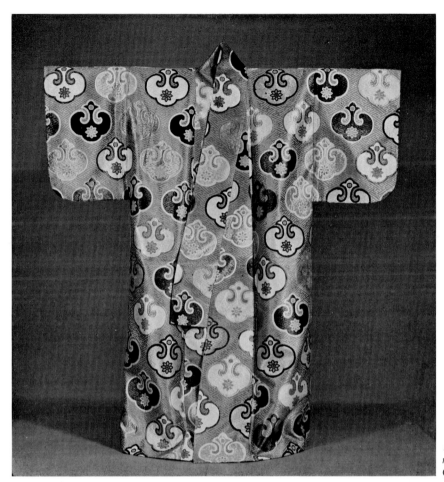

141. Unban *(cloud-shaped gong) motif. Nō costume; Edo period. Okura Museum, Tokyo.*

developed a great number of variations. As one example, the metal fittings used to ornament household furnishings such as door handles, nailhead covers, chests of drawers, and the like assumed the shapes of such objects as *noshi* (thin folded strips of abalone, a symbol of prosperity), rice paddles, flower baskets (Plate 128), arrows, folding fans, gourds, and other very common objects.

Observation of Natural Phenomena

One outstanding motif based upon a natural phenomenon is the circular motif known variously as "snow ring" or "snow pattern." The great variety of hexagonal snowflake patterns was certainly derived from close observation of actual snowfalls. Other pop-

ular snow patterns of the Momoyama period, including the snow-laden willow in Plate 89, were adapted to the new taste of Edo-period urban citizens and appear frequently on kimono. The manner in which snow was formalized in a number of motifs, in combination with various plants or landscapes, can only be explained by the familiarity of the natural phenomenon, and is a particular expression of the Japanese feeling of intimacy with the beauty of nature.

Religious Motifs

Objects which originally had significance as religious symbols or which were implements associated with religious rituals gradually became, in the worldly atmosphere of the Edo period, patterns for use on secular objects. For example, the *rinbō* Buddhist "wheel of life," a basic emblem of the faith, and the *unban*, a cloud-shaped gong used in Zen monasteries, held a certain appeal for their formality and complexity of shape, and appeared frequently on the *kara-ori* and other textiles used in making Nō costumes (Plate 141).

Other Decorative Patterns

The vast array of Edo decorative motifs encompasses familiar themes drawn from classical literary works such as the twelfth-century *Tale of Genji* and the fourteenth-century *Tales of Ise*. Themes from popular folklore or from children's stories such as *Momotarō, the Peach Boy* or *Oni no Nembutsu (The Devil's Prayer)* appear quite commonly. Many Edo patterns were based on Chinese traditions, including the "three laughers of Tiger Valley" or Kanzan and Jittoku, the two eccentric T'ang monks who figure prominently in the Zen tradition. Other motifs were of annual festivals such as Sagichō (a ceremonial burning of calligraphy written at New Year's, held several weeks after the start of each year), Hatsu-uma (the first horse day, early in the second month), Boy's Day (early in May), Tanabata (celebrated on the seventh night of the seventh month of the lunar calendar), and the chrysanthemum festival in the autumn. Scenic spots such as the "Eight Views of the Hsiao and Hsiang Rivers" (a popular Chinese theme taken up in Japanese painting), or the "Three Famous Scenic Spots in Japan" (Matsushima, Miyajima, and Ama-no-hashidate) were favorite themes of Edo decoration and were frequently combined with writing in the *ashide* device.

Many of the characteristic motifs of the Edo period could only have arisen in the heady, fashion-conscious atmosphere of the times. No less numerous than the distinctly Edo motifs, however, are the traditional designs which continued to be used or which, having once died out, were enthusiastically revived. As life styles changed and patterns of thought and taste changed with them, novel motifs that were considered radical or delightfully avant-garde were constantly in demand. On the other hand, motifs deeply rooted in the spirit of tradition, by adapting slightly to the particular requirements of the time, could still maintain their ageless fascination. In this manner, decorative motifs were inextricably entwined with the lives of the people using them, and grew and changed with the times.

In the middle of the nineteenth century, the feudal political structure of the Tokugawa shogunate was supplanted by the new government that accompanied the restoration of the person of the emperor to authority. Emperor Meiji, who assumed the throne in 1867, was the first ruler of Japan's modern period, and during his reign Japan launched its era of "Western cultural enlightenment." Notwithstanding the enormous political and cultural changes that have occurred in Japan during the past century, traditional design motifs continue to enhance the lives of the Japanese people.

9

Yūsoku Textile Patterns

The general term *yūsoku* refers refers to the ancient customs and ceremonies of the Japanese court, and the study of *yūsoku* extends to all aspects of ancient court life, from laws and ordinances and forms of government procedure to dress, personal ornamentation, and domestic furnishings. "*Yūsoku* patterns," however, refer specifically to the textile designs which developed at the Heian court for use on the garments worn on ceremonial occasions.

Not a single original costume dating from the Heian period exists today. Fortunately, however, the woven textile patterns known as *yūsoku* patterns, with their origins in the costume motifs of the Heian period, provide the basis for an imaginative reconstruction of traditional dress. From the middle of the Heian period onward, the Japanese nobility abandoned the T'ang-influenced dress that had prevailed theretofore; clothing worn at court regained a Japanese flavor and became increasingly voluminous and multilayered. Similarly, the *hōsōge* patterns and animal motifs of Chinese origin that had appeared on the dyed fabrics of the Nara period gradually disappeared, and use of multicolored *nishiki* brocade also died out. Replacing them were solid-color silk textiles with designs expressed solely by contrasting weaves. Due largely to technical necessity, woven patterns tend to be geometrical. In order to decorate fabrics with more complex, pictorial designs, the technique of double-layer weaves was perfected. This allowed weavers to produce patterns of birds and flowers in soft, harmonious colors on

142. Yūsoku *pattern: peony motif.*

143. Yūsoku *pattern:* koaoi *(hollyhock) motif.*

expansively-patterned woven textiles that had the appearance of embroidery. At the same time, the thin materials used for summer wear preserved the techniques of *karami-ori* (gauze weaving) from the Nara period. These gauze textiles were characterized by an inventive use of various diamond patterns.

During the Kamakura period, the everyday dress of the aristocracy was further simplified, and garments which until then had been used only for daily wear at home became acceptable for formal appearances at court and in other ceremonial rituals. Such newly elevated everyday wear included the *sokutai* (a nobleman's costume consisting of two voluminous over robes above a short jacket and baggy trousers) and the *karaginumo* (a short open-front cloak worn by court ladies and traditionally made of *karaginu* or Chinese brocade). Simultaneously, however, a formal etiquette of dress was codified. According to these rules, the fancy woven patterns on the outer coat of the *sokutai* and elsewhere were strictly dictated by rank, and certain patterns were reserved to the exclusive use of particular families. It is these standardized motifs that have been passed down as *yūsoku* patterns.

Each of the *yūsoku* motifs came originally to Japan from China during the Nara period, but became thoroughly established in Japanese usage and gradually took on the characteristics of Japanese taste, finally losing all marked differences from other native decorative patterns. In the course of their continuous usage up to the present day, they have inevitably incorpo-

144. *An early seventeenth-century kimono that illustrates magnificently the application of* yūsoku *patterns to Edo-period textiles. Medallions comprised of wisteria blossoms curved into the* tomoe *motif of two linked "commas" are superimposed on a rich ground of* kikko-hanabishi *(floral rhombus enclosed in tortoise-shell lattice). Tokyo National Museum.*

rated some motifs which postdate the Heian period. Still, *yūsoku* may well be considered one of the primary sources of Japanese design motifs.

Tasuki Pattern

Consisting of straight lines, intersecting on the diagonal to form a diamond-shaped lattice, the *tasuki* pattern is the most natural and basic geometric pattern in woven textiles. The name is derived from the *tasuki*, which is a loop of cloth used since earliest times to bind up kimono sleeves by slipping it under each arm and crossing it in the back. The x-shaped cross thus produced has given its name to many intersecting-line

motifs. Triple lines intersecting on the diagonal, with or without diamonds fitted into the interstices, are known as "triple *tasuki*." An overall pattern of diamonds, the space around them simulating the *tasuki* lattice, is called "diamond *tasuki*." Birds fitted into the *tasuki* lattice produce the "bird *tasuki*" (Plate 145). There are numerous other variations, such as the overall arrangement of diamonds with slightly concave edges known as "pine-needle *tasuki*."

Diamond Pattern

The *tasuki* lattice pattern defines diamond-shaped spaces, and many of the *tasuki* patterns may well be

145. Yūsoku *patterns. Top, left to right:* paulownia, bamboo, and phoenix *motif;* phoenix on a ground of *koaoi;* clouds enclosed in tate-waku *pattern. Bottom, left to right: bird* tasuki *motif; clouds and cranes motif;* ka *motif on an* ishi-datami *ground.*

thought of as diamond patterns, in terms of space rather than lines. Other variants of the diamond motif include triple diamonds one within the other, clusters of four diamonds grouped in a large diamond outline, "auspicious diamonds" (four foliate diamonds clustered in a diamond-shaped arrangement), diamonds enclosing Chinese-style ornate floral motifs (*karahana*), and diamond-shaped outlines framing confronting butterflies or confronting birds. The name *shigebishi* (diamond thicket) is given to a diamond-shaped tight lattice pattern with thick and thin lines. A similar arrangement, but one in which the diamonds are not contiguous, is known as *tōbishi* (distant diamonds), and is identical to the diamond *tasuki* pattern.

Tatewaku Pattern

The *tatewaku* pattern consists of parallel undulating lines arranged regularly along the warp (*tate*) of the textile so that adjacent lines define oval lozenges (Plate 145). The name, meaning "rising boil," probably comes from the pattern's resemblance to rising billows of steam. Scrolled clouds, wisteria tendrils, *karahana*, honeysuckle, and other patterns inserted in the lozenges give their respective names to particular types of *tatewaku*. In the Nō-drama *kosode* kimono illustrated in Plate 102, the *tatewaku* motif forms a rhythmically unifying backdrop to an elaborately embroidered pattern of lilies and imperial carriages.

Karakusa Pattern

Within the general *karakusa* category of arabesque or scrolling vine pattern are included peony, gentian, seedling pine, melon, and clove motifs. The bridle-bit *karakusa* is frequently found on formal coats.

Koaoi Pattern

The *koaoi* is a formal pattern based on a flower very similar to the peony or to the floral rhombus called *hanabishi*. In Plate 145, the *koaoi* provides the background for the more prominent flying phoenix motif. This "small hollyhock" motif that appears among *yūsoku* patterns should not be confused with the *aoi* or hollyhock motif that became popular during the Edo period.

Kikkō Pattern

The hexagonal lattice pattern called *kikkō* (tortoise shell) was used with great frequency after the beginning of the Heian period. It was often used to enclose flower motifs (Plate 55 and 144), in which case it is called *kikkō-hanabishi* (tortoise-shell lattice with floral rhombus), and frequently formed the background pattern for large medallions in various types of brocade.

Paulownia, Bamboo, Phoenix, and Kirin Pattern

A design motif established during the Heian period shows a phoenix flying above paulownia trees, which were traditionally believed to be the fabled bird's roosting place (Plate 145). In some versions, bamboo is also added. In the late Heian or Kamakura period, the *kirin*, another auspicious mythological beast, was added to the group, and the resulting motif was reserved primarily for use on the emperor's outer garments.

Ishi-datami Pattern

The *ishi-datami*, or "paving stone," pattern takes its name from the tile or flagstone floors in Chinese-style palaces and covered passageways between buildings. On *yūsoku* textiles, its alternate name is *arare* or "hailstone." The pattern is produced by raised woof threads, and other motifs are frequently produced on the warp threads in the interstices. In Plate 145, the

ishi-datami pattern forms the barely visible background for the *ka* motif (see below).

Wachigai Pattern

This pattern of interlocking circles of identical diameter to form an overall chain-mail pattern was also known, from the Edo period on, as the *shippō-tsunagi* (seven linked jewels) motif. In floral *wachigai* patterns, small four-petaled flowers are inserted in each circle.

Medallion Pattern

Medallion patterns consist of wisteria, cranes, butterflies, waves, *karahana* and so forth, arranged in circular shapes with a clearly defined border. Occasionally, pairs of objects or animals such as facing cranes or facing butterflies are adapted to a medallion arrangement. An alternate name for an all-over pattern of large medallions is *fusenryō* (floating-line brocade), so called after the characteristic designs formed by loose, floating threads in a special weaving technique.

Ka Pattern

The *ka* motif is said to be based upon a circular section of papaya fruit, and the most characteristic applications of the motif pair it with a floral rhombus (Plate 145). The standard pattern for the outermost layer of *hakama* or full trailing trousers worn by noblemen was the *ka* pattern set on an *ishi-datami* or *arare* ground.

Phoenix Pattern

The oldest existing *uchiki* or everyday kimono of the ancient court dates from the Kamakura period and is preserved at the Tsurugaoka Hachiman Shrine in Kamakura. It exhibits a pattern of phoenixes worked in raised threads and placed at random on a *koaoi* ground (Plate 145).

Other Patterns

Motifs of mist, gnarled trees, and *suhama* (stylized sandbar design) appear on fabric used for clothing, particularly in women's court robes, and for covering screens. Another fairly common pattern has flying cranes spaced at regular intervals among clusters of stylized clouds (Plate 145).

10

Family Crests

In the *monshō* or hereditary crests of Japanese families can be seen the distillation of many of the basic design motifs of Japanese arts and crafts. The crests shared similar origins and the same historical development as the other motifs discussed in this book, but by their highly simplified nature they reduce common motifs to their essential components. Historically, the crests were the insignia of noted families and were used to mark the formal kimono, household utensils, lanterns, and gravestones of a particular house. Some extensive families maintained a number of crests, and as households split or were divided into branches, variations of the original crest were devised for the branch families. In modern Japan, the high degree of fragmentation of extended families into numerous separate nuclear families has tended to lessen the social significance of crests. And yet, the crests themselves remain as examples of outstanding design. Furthermore, as their function as family symbols declined, crests have been used increasingly by commercial organizations and large businesses, not unlike the trade marks by which Western manufacturers identify their products.

Origins of Family Crests

Monshō have played an important role in Japanese society as marks representing both nobility and commoners, but the crests of the various social classes developed out of markedly different circumstances. During the Heian period, crests were used in aristocratic society to mark the ox-carts of each household, serving as both identification and ornament. So, too, as

146. *Family crests; Edo and Meiji periods. Top row:* ishi-datami *(paving stone) and* inazuma *(lightning bolt) motifs. Bottom row:* wachigai *(interlocking rings) and* tomoe *(rotating commas) motifs.*

ornamental motifs on clothing, generations of a given family favored particular patterns: the Konoe family, which traced its lineage back into Japanese antiquity, adopted the peony, while the Saionji noble house was partial to the *tomoe* or "comma" pattern. During the early Kamakura period, these favored motifs became established as insignia on the *hō* or formal outer robe. In this manner, the insignia on carriages and clothing gradually came to be recognized as the symbol of a particular household, representing the position, taste, and honor of the family. The motifs selected were intricate, meaningful, and of great elegance.

In the case of military families, there was need on the battlefields during the incessant wars for insignia on banners and on armor to distinguish friend from foe, and to provide footsoldiers with a symbol around which to rally their zeal. Crests became symbolic devices for representing the unity of a family. Under such circumstances, the crests themselves had to be simple, legible, and clearly recognizable. The earliest insignia were often simple ideograms based on straight lines or circles, written with a brush. Other crests were graphic stylizations of certain objects.

By the end of the Kamakura period, such insignia had been adopted formally as the crests of leading families. The *Taiheiki,* a military chronicle of the early Muromachi period, refers to family crests instead of surnames, implying that the crests of certain important families were universally known. The chrysanthemum and paulownia, now the insignia of the imperial household, were originally used as common ornaments on garments and table utensils because of their auspicious significance; by the end of the Kamakura period, however, they were reserved for the emperor's ex-

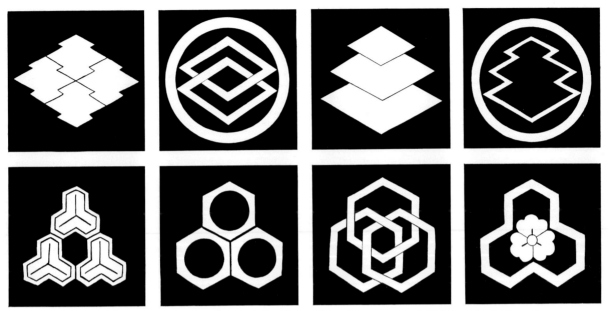

147. *Family crests; Edo and Meiji periods. Top row:* hishi *(diamond) motifs. Bottom row:* kikkō *(tortoise shell) motifs.*

clusive use. Aristocratic and powerful military families followed suit, adopting crests to lend an air of dignity to their clothing and possessions.

Transformation of Crests

During the civil wars in the late Kamakura and early Muromachi periods, when conflicting military allegiances splintered households, the need arose to distinguish the crests of offshoots of a single family and many variations developed out of the basic insignia. The number of motifs was also increasing, and realistic motifs were stylized and simplified for use as *monshō*.

During the Edo period, when it became customary to display either three or five crests at fixed spots on formal kimono, the designs became even more stylized and symmetrical, and they appeared almost universally in a medallion format. Moreover, as the need for battlefield identification disappeared, crests became important primarily as emblems of status: hierarchies were strictly codified under the Japanese feudal system, and the crests displayed on vehicles and clothing were a quick means of identifying rank in order to accord the bearer of the crest the appropriate privileges he might be due. Handbooks of crests were guides to insignia of daimyo and others in the highest ranks of society. Edo-period *bukan* (books of heraldry) and other catalogues listed the surname, crest, and landholdings of each daimyo and government official and were revised annually until the abolishment of the clans by the Meiji government in 1871.

The Edo period was a time of extended peace, and the crests of the military families tended to be used mainly for ornamental purposes. As decorative crests

148. Family crests; Edo and Meiji periods. Top row: hanabishi *(flower diamond) motifs. Bottom row:* ichō *(gingko leaf) motifs.*

replaced older versions, basic insignia were increasingly embellished; numerous variations appeared and the names of the crests also became more elaborate. This tendency was most marked during the late seventeenth and early eighteenth centuries, when Japanese society as a whole was intensely preoccupied with fashion, elegance, and personal adornment.

Merchant Society and Family Crests

During the Edo period, merchant families were able, within the limitations of sumptuary legislation, to accumulate a certain amount of power based on wealth rather than social status. Many became avid patrons of the arts, the theatre, and the so-called "floating world" of the licensed quarters. Vanity and self-esteem also led rich merchant families to begin

adopting crests. Unlike the more reserved and austere aristocratic and military houses, merchant households tended to be aggressive and flamboyant, and their crests were not the orthodox *kamon* (household crests) but were called *date-mon* (dandyish or foppish crests). These frequently were eclectic designs based upon historical events or famous places; others were developed from traditional merchant talismans for business prosperity or from visual puns and picture puzzles related to the business of the family or the products it dealt in. Many of these novel crests were rendered in several colors, in which case they were known as "Kaga crests" from the frequent use of colored crests by the households of Kaga Province. Sometimes lovers would combine the insignia of both their families into a composite crest called *hiyoku-mon*. The tastemakers in the designing of such informal crests were actors and ladies

149. Family crests; Edo and Meiji periods. Top row: ume *(plum blossom) motifs. Bottom row:* tsuru *(crane) and* take *(bamboo) motifs.*

of leisure. Even modern heraldry books show over one hundred twenty crests belonging to actors and theatrical families. Many are derived from personal names or from visual puns on the personal names of actors.

Among merchants there was also the custom of devising easily recognizable insignia for the firm or shop by taking one character from the name of the owner or founder and enclosing it in a circle, square, or hexagon. Variations might have the first character of the founder's name placed beneath an inverted L-shaped bracket, representing a carpenter's square and symbolizing wealth. Just as the crests of the military families had flown on banners carried into battle, the merchant insignia were dyed on shop curtains or carved on signboards hung outside the shop. In a sense, these were the battleflags of the merchants' world and symbolized the pride of hereditary com-

mercial establishments that were denied military or political position in the rigid social hierarchy. It was also customary for servants to wear their master's crest on their work clothes and for employees to use their master's crest. For this purpose, large decorative versions of the crest were dyed on the center back and the front collar of the work jackets that have come to be known in the West as "happi-coats." In general, these crests were of powerful, bold composition, containing all the dash and wit that characterized the merchant attitudes toward life and work. Some two hundred such merchant motifs are listed in modern heraldry books.

Motifs and Composition of Crests

The countless number of crest motifs can be clas-

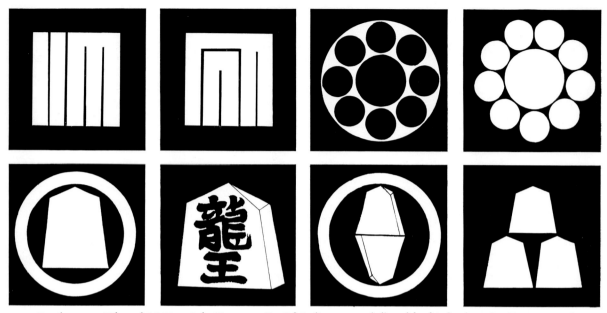

150. *Family crests; Edo and Meiji periods. Top row:* Genji-kō *(incense symbol) and* hoshi *(star) motifs. Bottom row:* koma *(chesspiece) motifs.*

sified generally into the following categories: plants, animals, natural phenomena, household utensils, architectural ornaments, geometric patterns, ideograms, religious symbols, and schematized motifs. Many of these, such as flowers, cranes, and tortoises or ideograms meaning "heaven," "prosperity," "good fortune," and the like, are chosen for their beauty or auspicious meaning. Frequently, one character will be borrowed from the family surname. Many military families devised crests by combining a sword with a traditional design motif such as *hanabishi* or *tomoe*, or by incorporating emblems of fortitude or warlike prowess such as falcons or weapons. Some families adopted emblems traditionally associated with their ancestral shrine: the deer of Kasuga Shrine, the monkeys of Hiyoshi Shrine, or the pigeons of Hachiman Shrine, all considered to be messengers of the gods;

other motifs of this type were the cedars of the sacred Mt. Miwa, the bamboo-and-oak motif of Kumano and Kasuga Shrines, or the double-leaf hollyhock emblem of Kumano Shrine. Other crests show architectural elements associated with shrines: *torii* gates, ornamental gable cross-beams, sacred Shinto ropes, handbells, or votive pictures. It was also common to commemorate in a simple crest symbols of the famous deeds or renowned ancestors or some indication of their birthplaces.

Originally, all members of one family used the same crest, but as the numbers of descendants proliferated over the generations, it became necessary to distinguish between main and branch families; this led to numerous variations derived from the identical original crest. Even in heraldic lists published after the Meiji Restoration, some 4500 variations are shown. In general, the

151. Family crests; Edo and Meiji periods. Top row: kari *(goose) motifs. Bottom row:* ji *(ideograph) motifs.*

following basic rules apply to the variations:

1. Adding a square or round border to the original crest; adding a corolla or vine to the original shape.

2. Reworking the original motif. Departing from the original drawn in thin lines, called the *yōmon* or "light crest," by

a. drawing the design with double lines to make a *kagemon* or "shadow crest";

b. showing the reverse side of the motif, such as the stem side rather than the face of a plum or chrysanthemum blossom;

c. changing from simple to complex, as from a single plum blossom to a double plum blossom;

d. creating a marked contrast of sharp and soft lines, as by sharpening the edges of the ivy or paulownia leaf to form "devil ivy" or "devil paulownia";

e. transforming a schematized representation into a pictorial one, such as the "Kōrin plum" crest;

f. changing the angle from which a motif is viewed or altering its manner of arrangement, such as showing a flower in full face or side view or turning it upside down;

g. bending or folding the original shape, as in the "folded oak" crest;

h. twisting the basic shape, as in the twisted plum blossom crest;

i. interlocking elements of the design;

j. adding new elements to the original motif, such as arrows added to a cart motif or wisteria to a *tomoe* pattern;

k. rearranging the elements of the basic motif, as in the *meyui* motifs made up of groups of squares arranged in various ways.

3. Doubling the original motif, making a pair of what was once one representation of the motif, as in the various gingko-leaf crests (Plate 148, bottom row). Pairs of the basic element can be shown facing each other, wrapped around each other, or crossing. In groups of three, the basic elements can be shown lined up, overlapping, arranged on top of each other, facing toward the center of the crest, facing out of the crest, or intertwining in a circular movement. Two identical crests may be linked by various devices, such as interlocking elements or overlapping borders. After marriage, a husband's crest and his wife's were frequently combined into a single new crest. Sometimes persons of high rank would allow their crests to be combined with those of retainers.

4. Isolating the elements of a complex crest by separating the component parts or by reassembling them in new fashion.

5. Abbreviating the elements of a complex crest, as in changing the *kuyō* nine-circle motif related to astrology into similar crests with fewer circles.

As suggested by the high degree of variation among crests, these family symbols were not rigidly established. Rather, they were sometimes granted as reward for service, bequeathed, exchanged, and frequently transferred. From the late Kamakura period on, there are numerous examples of a man's adopting a vanquished enemy's crest or of an inferior's usurping the crest of a man of higher rank. During the Edo period, "alternate crests" were designed for private or incognito use.

Considered from the point of view of design, it is clear that the Kamakura period was the first highly creative era in the development of Japanese crests. Kamakura designs tended to be pictorial and asymmetrical. By the end of the Muromachi period, they had become more regular, schematic, and symmetrical. Most Edo period crests were contained within a circular border, and purely ornamental crests finally became a part of the lives of commoners as well as the aristocracy.

Today, most formal crests dating from earlier eras are preserved in contemporary books of heraldry, while *date-mon*, the informal crests taken on by commoners and merchants, are to be found in such sources as contemporary handbooks of towel designs, and appear even today as trade marks or as ornamentation. Although most crests have lost the significance they once had, they continue to fascinate us with their endless ingenuity, freshness, and originality of design.

Glossary

akigusa: various autumn flowers and grasses, especially popular as motifs for *maki-e* inlaid lacquer

arare (hailstone): pattern of small, evenly spaced squares; an alternate name for *ishi-datami* on *yūsoku* textiles (see also *ishi-datami, ka*)

ashide: originally, a loose, flowing style of calligraphic ideogram inserted into a picture to resemble reeds, whirlpools, tree roots, or branches; hence, any design in which ideograms or phonetic symbols are made to serve as part of a natural landscape (see also *uta-e*)

atsuita: stiff brocade with twilled ground, frequently used in Nō costumes

aya: plain color twill-weave silk, often used as ground for raised woven patterns

ban-e: medallion motif used on textiles, classical dance costumes, and furnishings during the Heian period

bingata: multicolor stencil-dyed textile from the Ryūkyū Islands, popular in Japan during the Edo period

chayatsuji: bleached hemp cloth dyed predominantly in indigo by means of rice-paste resist method, usually with a landscape design, and used for summer kimono. During the Edo period, *chayatsuji* textiles were sometimes further ornamented with embroidery and used for women's wear in high-ranking families.

chinkin (sunken gold): a Chinese method of lacquer ornamentation brought to Japan in the Muromachi period. Thin strips of gold foil are pressed into finely carved contours in the lacquer surface.

Edo komon: small allover stencil-dyed textile pattern, produced in Edo

fuse-saishiki: decorative technique in which the pattern or polychromed surface is partially concealed by an openwork covering of tortoise shell or crystal

fusenryō (floating-line textile): originally, a type of plain twill with designs superimposed in loose, floating threads; now designates any large medallion pattern of the type common on such textiles

fusuma: sliding doors separating the rooms of a Japanese house; usually made of heavy, opaque paper with painted decoration covering a wooden frame

habutae: soft plain woven silk resembling taffeta, produced by the Nishijin weavers since the Momoyama period

hanabishi (flower diamond): a diamond pattern with foliate edges; frequently combined with *kikkō* lattice (see also *kikkō hanabishi*)

hōju: Buddhist peach-shaped symbol of a round jewel with pointed top, sometimes ringed with flames; has the power to grant any wish

Hōrai-san: enchanted island of the Taoist immortals (Chinese: P'eng-lai Shan); an auspicious motif

hōsōge: floral motif used frequently in Buddhist ornamentation, featuring an imaginary flower possibly based on the peony

hōsōge karakusa: vine-scroll pattern incorporating imaginary *hōsōge* flowers (see *karakusa*)

ishi-datami (paving stone): checkerboard pattern, so called after stone floors in Chinese palaces; on *yūsoku* textiles also known as *arare*; also called "Ichimatsu pattern" after a 17th-century Kabuki actor who favored the design (see *arare*)

iokon: striated pattern on Jōmon-period pottery produced by scraping the damp clay surface with the edge of a scallop shell

jōmon: cord pattern on Jōmon-period pottery produced by rolling a cord-wrapped stick across the damp clay. The period takes its name from the pottery technique.

ka: stylized five-lobed floral medallion said to be based on the cross-section of a papaya

ka and arare: a common *yūsoku* pattern comprised of stylized floral medallions superimposed on a checkerboard ground

kaigara: shell pattern on Jōmon-period pottery produced by pressing scallop shells into the damp clay surface

Kamakura-bori: Chinese lacquer technique of carving relief designs into thick lacquer, usually in red or black, or layers of both colors. It flourished in Japan during the Kamakura period.

karabitsu: a small Chinese-style lacquer chest, mounted on four short legs in contrast to the flat-bottom Japanese chests

karahana (Chinese flower): an imaginary many-petaled floral motif

karahana tatewaku: design of *karahana* inserted between vertical wavy lines (see also *tatewaku*)

karakusa (Chinese grass): a scrolling vine motif introduced into Japan from T'ang China. Its basic shape is a continuous scrolling vine, not unlike the Western arabesque; often incorporated in the vine pattern are flowers, fruits, various leaves, butterflies and other insects.

kara-ori (Chinese weave): rich brocade with design in satin weave on twill woven ground, and lavishly embellished with gold and colored threads; used in costumes for Nō drama

karyōbinga (Sanskrit: *kalavinka*): Buddhist mythological figure originating in Indian folklore; half-bird, half-woman with bell-like voice, living in the Buddhist paradise

kasuri: splash-pattern weave with design produced by tie-dye in warp and woof threads before weaving. White geometric patterns on navy-blue ground are most common.

kataginu: stiff sleeveless jacket worn as costume in Kyōgen drama

katamigawari: "half-and-half" pattern for kimono in which the two halves of the garment are made of different fabrics or designs. A similar technique is used on Oribe ceramics.

kasanetsugi: a collage technique of mounting layered patches of torn papers on poetry sheets during the Heian period

kesadasuki: a lattice pattern resembling the bands on the *kesa* robes of Buddhist priests (see also *tasuki*)

kikkō (tortoise shell): a hexagonal lattice pattern, used singly or in clusters (as on crests), but more frequently as an overall ground pattern

kikkō hanabishi: foliate diamonds within the *kikkō* hexagonal lattice pattern, a very popular motif since the Heian period (see also *hanabishi, kikkō*)

kirikane (cut gold): the technique of applying gold leaf cut in decorative patterns, either geometric or floral, to Buddhist lacquer sculpture and painting

kirin: kylin, fabulous animal of composite form from Chinese mythology

koaoi: small, stylized eight-petal flower in formal arrangements, frequently used as ground pattern on brocaded textiles

kosode: women's everyday kimono with short hanging sleeves, worn since the late Heian period; also used as a costume in the Nō drama

kotobuki: ideogram meaning "long life and prosperity," often used as an element in various decorative patterns

kōzama: ornamental panel on dais of Buddhist altar

kuyō: motif deriving from Indian mythology, consisting of eight small circles arranged around a large central circle; introduced to Japan with esoteric Buddhism in the 9th century; also used as a crest motif (see also *rokuyō*)

maki-e: general term for decorations done with gold and silver pigment or metallic leaf on lacquer. The metallic pigment, powder or leaf, is spread on the lacquer before it dries. Mother-of-pearl is also frequently used in *maki-e*.

matsukawabishi (pine-bark diamond): a motif of three overlapping diamond shapes, the middle of which is the largest

meyui: textile pattern of hollow squares produced by tie-dyeing technique, formalized into a checkerboard pattern of squares standing on the diagonal; used frequently in family crests

namban (southern barbarians): the term generally applied to Westerners, initially to Portuguese and Spanish merchants and missionaries, who reached Japan from the East Indies in the mid-sixteenth century

neriginu: glossed silk produced by the Nishijin weavers beginning in the Momoyama period

nishiki (brocade): a term originally applied to any richly textured fabric regardless of weaving technique

noshi: thin folded strips of abalone or paper used as an ornament on auspicious occasions. The shape of the *noshi* itself became a decorative motif.

oshigata: pattern on Jōmon-period pottery produced by pressing various objects in the damp clay surface

rokuyō: motif derived from Indian astrology, consisting of five circles arranged around a larger central circle; frequently used as a crest motif (see also *kuyō*)

shibori-zome: tie-dyeing

shikishi: squares of tinted or decorated paper used for inscribing poetry

shippō tsunagi (seven linked jewels): an overall pattern consisting of interlocking circles named after the seven precious elements of Buddhism; on *yūsoku* textiles, the pattern is known also as *wachigai*

suhama: stylized "sandbar" motif, usually with three lobes, combined with naturalistic motifs as a purely formal shape

suminagashi (flowing ink): a marbleized pattern produced by dropping black ink on damp paper; frequently used in the Heian period on poetry sheets

sutra: Buddhist scriptures

tasuki: a geometric pattern consisting of straight lines intersecting on the diagonal to form a diamond lattice (see also *kesadasuki*)

tatewaku: overall pattern of vertical, evenly spaced undulating lines defining oval lozenges (see also *karahana tatewaku*)

tebako: a lidded lacquer box with several removable compartments, used by court ladies as a cosmetics case

temmon kosode: a type of elegant *kosode* kimono popular during the Momoyama period

tomoe: a motif comprised of two or three comma shapes united with heads together and tails revolving, forming a perfect circle

torii: ceremonial gateway to a Shinto shrine

tsuba: sword guard

tsujigahana: stitched tie-dyeing technique fashionable in the Muromachi period

uchiwa: round-faced fan mounted on a stiff bamboo frame; the fan shape was used frequently as a decorative motif

unban: originally a Chinese bronze gong, brought to Japan together with Zen Buddhism in the Kamakura period and used in Zen monasteries. Its shape is a popular motif for textiles and family crests.

ungen-saishiki: painting technique in which several gradations of color are juxtaposed to create an effect of depth. Perfected in T'ang China, this manner of painting is seen in Japanese Buddhist arts and architecture of the Nara and Heian periods.

uta-e: a design illustrating the meaning or feeling expressed in a *waka*, a thirty-one syllable poem (see also *ashide*)

wachigai: an interlocking circle motif, known also as *shippō tsunagi*

warabide: fernlike leaf pattern

yaburitsugi (torn patches): a Heian-style collage technique used to decorate poetry sheets

yori-ito: twine pattern on Jōmon-period pottery

Index

The "weathermark" identifies this English-
language edition as having been planned,
designed, and produced at the Tokyo offices of John Weatherhill, Inc.,
in collaboration with Shibundō Publishing Company. Book
design and typography by Dana Levy. Text composed by Kenkyūsha.
Engraving and printing by Hanshichi Printing Company.
Bound at Oguchi Binderies. The type of the main text is set
in 11-pt. Bembo with hand-set Goudy Bold for display.